PEER FEEDBACK
IN THE CLASSROOM

ASCD MEMBER BOOK

Many ASCD members received this book as a
member benefit upon its initial release.

Learn more at: **www.ascd.org/memberbooks**

PEER FEEDBACK IN THE CLASSROOM

EMPOWERING STUDENTS TO BE THE EXPERTS

STARR SACKSTEIN

ASCD

ALEXANDRIA, VIRGINIA

1703 N. Beauregard St. • Alexandria, VA 22311-1714 USA
Phone: 800-933-2723 or 703-578-9600 • Fax: 703-575-5400
Website: www.ascd.org • E-mail: member@ascd.org
Author guidelines: www.ascd.org/write

Deborah S. Delisle, *Executive Director;* Robert D. Clouse, *Managing Director, Digital Content & Publications;* Stefani Roth, *Publisher;* Genny Ostertag, *Director, Content Acquisitions;* Julie Houtz, *Director, Book Editing & Production;* Miriam Calderone, *Editor;* Donald Ely, *Senior Graphic Designer;* Mike Kalyan, *Director, Production Services;* Valerie Younkin, *Production Designer;* Kyle Steichen, *Senior Production Specialist*

All web links in this book are correct as of the publication date below but may have become inactive or otherwise modified since that time. If you notice a deactivated or changed link, please e-mail books@ascd.org with the words "Link Update" in the subject line. In your message, please specify the web link, the book title, and the page number on which the link appears.

PAPERBACK ISBN: 978-1-4166-2366-3   ASCD product #117020

PDF E-BOOK ISBN: 978-1-4166-2367-0; see Books in Print for other formats.

Quantity discounts are available: e-mail programteam@ascd.org or call 800-933-2723, ext. 5773, or 703-575-5773. For desk copies, go to www.ascd.org/deskcopy.

ASCD Member Book No. FY17-6B (Apr. 2017 PS). Member books mail to Premium (P), Select (S), and Institutional Plus (I+) members on this schedule: Jan, PSI+; Feb, P; Apr, PSI+; May, P; Jul, PSI+; Aug, P; Sep, PSI+; Nov, PSI+; Dec, P. For details, see www.ascd.org/membership and www.ascd.org/memberbooks.

Library of Congress Cataloging-in-Publication Data
Names: Sackstein, Starr, author.
Title: Peer feedback in the classroom : empowering students to be the experts / Starr Sackstein.
Description: Alexandria, Virginia, USA : ASCD, [2017] | Includes bibliographical references and index.
Identifiers: LCCN 2016057176 (print) | LCCN 2017006958 (ebook) | ISBN 9781416623663 (Paperback) | ISBN 9781416623670 (EBook)
Subjects: LCSH: Peer teaching.
Classification: LCC LB1031.5 .S24 2017 (print) | LCC LB1031.5 (ebook) | DDC 371.26--dc23
LC record available at https://lccn.loc.gov/2016057176

26 25 24 23 22 21 20 19 18 17   1 2 3 4 5 6 7 8 9 10 11 12

To my many student editors over the years, who taught me the power of relinquishing control and gave me faith in teenagers as trustworthy and responsible reporters.

PEER FEEDBACK IN THE CLASSROOM

Empowering Students to Be the Experts

FOREWORD

Margaret Mead's belief that "children must be taught how to think, not what to think" is one of the linchpins of the changing nature of schools in this century. We know with certainty that the body of knowledge we have built schools around is growing and changing. We can no longer say with confidence, "If you learn these subjects, you will be successful in life." What we *can* know with confidence is that success in life will depend on knowing how to think. This was true when Margaret Mead said it, and it's true today.

The business of educating children is a generative, complicated, and legislated endeavor. We have accepted a structure from the previous century. The practices and trends that exist in and around schools are old and clung to out of familiarity, past success, and hesitation to engage in the difficult discussions that inform decisions about what and how to change. The model that schools have followed for centuries is centered on bestowing bodies of knowledge in an established sequence and then assessing students' acquisition of that knowledge. Assessment has traditionally consisted of a combination of local assessments, observations, and standardized tests. But the world in which our schools were built—both in practice and architecturally—is no longer reflective of the world in which we and our students live today. As the current century continues to unfold, it is increasingly apparent that the old model is no longer effective, despite the fact that it remains overwhelmingly in place.

Children walk through the doors of our schools for the first time wide-eyed, excited, energetic, and filled with expectations, hope, and wonder—and that is what we wish to see in them for the next 13 years. So what is drained from these learners as the years go by? What brings them to the place where they say, "What do I need to do to pass?" "Why didn't you give me an *A*?" "I'm just not good at this!" and, worst of all, "I don't care"?

Numerous factors contribute to this decline, including those we have no control over, such as developmental stages. In this book, Starr Sackstein takes aim at the powerful intervening factors that we *do* have control over: how teaching takes place, and how teaching can lead to either energizing engagement or disappointing distraction. As educational leaders and teachers work together to decide how they can best educate today's students, the roles of the teacher and the student must change radically.

The call for change leadership is loud. In this century, there is wider recognition that leadership resides in many places across an organization—not just at the top. Recognizing and tapping the strength of the leaders throughout their schools will be the only way school leaders will be able to successfully lead change.

Starr is a practitioner and thought leader who leads from within the organization, applying her innovative practices with her students. Her experiences give her a unique understanding of the challenges and possibilities of peer feedback. Her writing in this book is humble and realistic. Whether one believes it can or cannot be achieved, this book not only lays out a path toward success, but also reflects the practice that takes place in her classroom with her students.

The shift of the teacher's role from "sage on the stage" to "guide on the side" has been gaining momentum in recent decades, and incorporating peer feedback into the classroom is a powerful way to initiate this shift. One path to empowering students as learners through peer feedback begins at the feet of school leaders as they invest in creating school environments of trust, where feedback is skilled and welcomed, and growth in practice is noted and celebrated. The other path can begin in teachers' classrooms. When enough teachers follow the journey that Starr shares in her writing, and the number of classrooms empowering students through this process grows, we can reach the tipping point.

The goal of empowering students as learners is a lofty one most everyone shares. But as with all things in education, it will work best when it takes systemic root. From a student's perspective, imagine the experience of being a peer feedback partner in one grade and then having that power taken away in the next grade, or in another class. Ultimately, a systemic buy-in to the concept and practice is essential.

The journey that led Starr to write this book reveals an unfolding, a revelation of the changing landscape of empowering and motivating students as active and curious learners. She began by shifting from grading students to offering them feedback, resulting in more engaged, active learners. She developed her own feedback skills and nurtured a new culture in her classes where students reflected on their work, sought advice, accepted and applied that advice, and took pride in their own development. What educator doesn't yearn for students to act in that way?

It would have been tempting to stop there; the work it took to arrive at that place was Herculean. But the goal of student empowerment must be an evolving one. The horizon changes depending on the spot where we are standing. Having arrived at this successful place, Starr saw that giving feedback rather than grades was still putting her in the position of sage on the stage, keeping the power and direction in her hands. She decided that some of it, at least, should be transferred to the students themselves.

Starr has graciously captured her journey toward this ever-moving horizon in her blog posts, articles, and books. Now she has arrived at a new place, ready to release even more responsibility to her students by teaching them the skills they need to be able to give and receive feedback. There is an educator's trick deeply set in this action. In order for students to learn how to give feedback, they have to know, recognize, and be able to speak to the elements of their work, whether it's a piece of writing, a top-notch lab report, a clear and correct math solution, a perfect pole vault, an exceptional oratory, or an exemplary explanation. The point is, in order for students to give feedback, they must know the elements of the standard and how to recognize and verbalize them while offering suggestions for next steps. In order for students to be prepared to receive feedback, the classroom culture must be one of respect and responsibility, sensitivity and empathy. These things must be in place before entering the peer feedback arena.

To truly benefit from this book, the reader must be prepared to go through this process carefully. Expecting students to plunge into peer feedback when the teacher has not been engaged in the peer feedback process him- or herself is not likely to lead to success. Begin at the beginning. As the chapters unfold, take each step carefully, as Starr challenges assumptions, reflects, and invites courageous trial and error. Then you, too, will be able to move toward the horizon where students are engaged, motivated, collaborative, creative, thoughtful communicators. Who wouldn't want that?

Jill Berkowicz
Coauthor, *The STEM Shift*
Adjunct Professor in Educational Leadership at SUNY New Paltz

ACKNOWLEDGMENTS

Scholastic journalism, at its heart, is about students being responsible reporters. We teach them to take control of their learning and then to share it with one another and the world. I'm deeply appreciative of the opportunity to teach journalism and advise a student publication. It is an honor to empower students in this most tangible and authentic setting.

I am grateful to the many folks who made this book possible.

To my friend and mentor Jill Berkowicz: you are always ready to help me with anything. I so greatly appreciate your guidance and wisdom. Thanks for being a part of this project and continuing to have my back.

A big thank you to the Journalism Education Association, the first professional organization where I really felt at home. To every member who has helped me grow as an adviser and a teacher: I am grateful for your generosity.

Thanks to Ardhys DeLeon and Deborah Kosnar, two former editors-in-chief and students who are now friends. I asked for your help, and you said yes without hesitation. I admire you as people, women, and change makers. Thank you for never being afraid to work with me.

A big thank you to a great group of current WJPS students: Alyssa Striano, Kahyun Kim, Barbara Kasomenakis, Hannah Zeitner, Nicole Kuliyev, and Helena Yeung. I asked for your input, and you shared fully.

Twitter has helped me connect with amazing educators around the world, and from these connections I was fortunate enough to meet and work with Rachel Rauch, Shelly Stephens, Ross Cooper, and Doug Robertson. I put out the bat signal, and you all responded. I'm so grateful and proud to have you be a part of this project.

As always, a special thank you to my friend and mentor Dr. Michael Curran, who is always ready to offer me fresh eyes and honest feedback.

Finally, thank you to all my students, present and past, who have taken what they know, taught it to one another, and used it to provide a service to their readers. Understanding the seriousness of the job they've been entrusted with, they have never let me or themselves down.

INTRODUCTION

Feedback. It's the moment in the learning process when students get the most personalized instruction possible. Between acknowledgment of what has improved and strategies provided for further improvement, what educators say and how we say it deeply influences the progress of each student.

Various educational researchers have explored the cognitive benefits of using feedback as a part of learning and found that effective feedback enhances both the giver's and the receiver's learning and development (see Brookhart, 2008). John Hattie's article "Feedback in Schools" (2012a) discusses in depth the research around intentional feedback, including its benefits and the specifics of how to do it well. Note the word *intentional*; this is key. In her book *Grit* (2016), Angela Duckworth discusses the necessity of intentional practice and goal setting to better inform feedback and mastery growth.

In my own experience as a classroom teacher, getting feedback on my performance from administration, colleagues, and even myself after viewing video recordings of my lessons has enabled me to pinpoint areas of needed growth and move forward with specific strategies in those areas, later repeating the feedback loop to ensure continued improvement.

Now imagine empowering *students* to provide one another with this type of feedback.

The Power of Peer Feedback

For a long time, I thought it was my sole responsibility to provide feedback to students. Arrogantly, I believed that I was the only one who could do the job properly. (After all, I'm the one with the degree, right?)

Time is the greatest teacher. Having taught many wonderful students over the years, I've learned that student-to-student feedback is often received more positively than teacher-to-student feedback. With basic instruction and ongoing support, students can learn to be exceptional peer strategists, providing thoughtful insight into what works from an audience's perspective and offering constructive strategies for improvement.

A side benefit of empowering students to provide feedback to one another is the awareness they themselves gain as learners. Teaching is perhaps the ultimate expression of learning. Providing students with regular opportunities to give and receive peer feedback enriches their learning experiences in powerful ways.

How This Book Came About

As a media adviser, I used to facilitate my school's online media outlet's content and revision process—until I realized that letting students run the show would provide an exceptional learning experience. Now, student reporters come up with the ideas for stories and submit drafts to student editors who, in turn, provide initial and follow-up feedback. Throughout the process of readying a piece for publication on the website, at least four student leaders work with each student reporter, ensuring optimal development of stories and student reporting skills as well as accuracy of content for a wide reading audience.

Delegating control to students has freed me up to conduct individual conferences with students who need more targeted help with their writing. These conferences yield further information to relay to the student leaders, who can use it to better serve the student reporters. Ensuring that the student leaders are armed with what they need to look for and how best to advise the other students to proceed is an important part of the process.

My experience transforming a school newspaper from a faculty-led publication to a student-led enterprise led me to realize the value of incorporating peer feedback into *any* class. And thus this book was born.

How This Book Is Organized

My goal with this book is to help you pass the power to students and provide them with the tools they need to give meaningful feedback to one another while you gather the data *you* need to provide appropriate instruction within a workshop-style classroom. Workshops, which are key to the approach outlined in this book, provide students with mini-lessons specifically aligned to success criteria and then have students put their learning directly into practice. This student-centered approach provides time for students to work cooperatively and independently as well as for the teacher to address different levels of need more flexibly throughout the class period.

I have divided the book into three parts. Chapters 1–3 explore the power of feedback and what meaningful feedback looks like in the classroom. Chapters 4 and 5 will help you prepare students for and introduce them to the feedback process. Chapters 6 and 7 address the nuts and bolts of peer feedback. I have included extended reflections from experienced practitioners of peer feedback that express, in students' and teachers' own words, the approach's powerful effect on learning and teaching.

Envision a classroom where all students work cooperatively to further their own learning and have the time and space to work with classmates who need help that used to be given only by the teacher. Sound good? Then you'll be excited to know that it not only is possible but also will change the way teaching and learning happen in your classroom.

PART 1

THE POWER OF FEEDBACK

1

THE RATIONALE FOR TEACHING STUDENTS TO PROVIDE PEER FEEDBACK

For too long, learners have been robbed of opportunities to exercise agency in their own learning. The traditional system that sets students up as subordinates to the teacher in the room makes it nearly impossible for them to truly own their learning. In this paradigm, the teacher is the one who has the power to issue strategies and feedback while the students are stuck waiting for the teacher to provide it. Unfortunately, in classrooms that usually contain one teacher to at least 20 students, students often have a long wait.

Imagine how the dynamic would change if we empowered all of the students in the room to provide meaningful feedback. Students would no longer need to wait passively to learn but be able to take responsibility for and actively move forward in their own learning process. This chapter explores why we should give students a greater role in their own learning—and the elements that need to be in place to do so.

Peer Feedback Empowers Students to Be Experts

Every student has the potential to be an expert. Our first job in the classroom is to get to know our students so that we can identify and expand on their strengths, in the process empowering and teaching them to be effective peer experts. Every content area or topic offers different opportunities for students to shine. By giving students the responsibility to share their expertise with one another, we are engaging them in the highest level of learning: asking them to teach. This mode of teaching and learning also naturally differentiates the learning because each student brings his or her own perspective, ideas, and preferences. Students see firsthand that there's no single "right" way to learn or teach.

There is no longer a need for teachers to be the only experts in the room. In fact, with the plethora of resources available online, the way we learn has changed so much that it isn't uncommon for students to know more about certain topics than teachers do. This fact shouldn't be threatening but exciting, as it opens up new opportunities for students and teachers to learn together.

Let's say a student in your class has a particular aptitude for technology and created a beautiful project using iMovie or Prezi. As a teacher, you were blown away by the artistry of the final project, but you feel ill equipped to teach other students to use the tool. Rather than freak out or force yourself through a crash course, why not ask that student to lead a Lunch and Learn session or even a class lesson on the technology? Empower the student to share his or her expertise for the benefit of the whole. Everyone wins, and students grow to see their teacher as a person who is open to suggestions—a stark contrast to the traditional role of the teacher.

This shift isn't necessarily easy or instantaneous. In fact, just as it can be difficult for teachers to cede control, students may find it hard to take control. To create a classroom of experts, you'll need to instill qualities of independence and self-advocacy in your students, a cumulative process that takes time to yield results.

Building Independence

Empowering students as experts means that they need to gain some control of their learning. The traditional education system tends to break down natural curiosity, training students to behave and learn in a way that prioritizes what's best for teachers over what's best for kids. Often, teachers control too much in the classroom, rendering students paralyzed and struggling to generate their own inquiry.

By contrast, cultivating an atmosphere that encourages "failing forward"—that is, one that sees mistakes as opportunities for growth rather than as closed-ended failures—increases students' engagement and awareness of their strengths and challenges and opens up endless opportunities for students and teachers alike to grow. Such an environment builds trust in and enthusiasm for the entire learning process rather than just the topic of the moment. It makes learning exciting by opening it up to infinite possibilities.

By creating classroom cultures that embody these qualities, educators can develop confident risk takers who are interested in innovation and in developing their own minds in ways that work for them. By cultivating individual growth in addition to covering content, teachers can give students the chance to follow their ideas and collaborate without fear of retribution or failure.

Developing Self-Advocacy

With a growing culture of independence, educators also need to instill in students a sense of self-advocacy—that they must know themselves and push to get their needs met in the ways that work best for them. This doesn't lessen the importance of the teacher's role, although some may see it that way; on the contrary, teachers are more important than ever in this context. They will be addressing students' specific needs whenever they arise rather than delivering wholesale, one-size-fits-all instruction.

Self-advocacy skills can be taught, and they should be as soon as students enter school in kindergarten. Along with questioning in general, these are crucial skills that will serve students well throughout their lives. As advocates for their own learning, students should know when they need help and how to get it. The teacher's role is to be receptive by providing help in ways that meet students' individual learning preferences. Thus, the teacher's goal is twofold: first to make sure that students can articulate their needs and then to try to meet those needs to the best of his or her ability.

Peer Feedback Fosters Growth

Because feedback is a reciprocal process, only a truly self-aware student can effectively evaluate peers and provide feedback. The relationship between the giver and the receiver of feedback develops both students as learners, helping them become more astute judges of their own learning. Asking the right questions, sharing information, identifying challenges, and providing strategies all work together to deepen students' mastery.

Traditionally, the teacher has been the sought-after expert in the classroom, the only person capable of providing students with the feedback they need. If we shift our mindset, we realize that we have *many* experts in the room who can help peers along in their learning. We can teach students to ask clarifying questions or point out inconsistencies, but the really important part is teaching the student who is asking for help to be specific in what he or she is looking to gain from the feedback.

One of my students reflected that asking her peers for help was a great way to grow:

> While working on this assignment, I was able to complete some of the following skill levels. During the week, we were asked to partner up with a peer and peer-review each other's plays. This skill allowed me to develop my honesty and understanding of what others can write and how others see my work. By sending someone else my play and reading theirs, I was able to get some new ideas off of them, and they pointed out my mistakes.

Giving students this responsibility is not without its pitfalls. Students don't always step up to the challenge and may falter in their ability to help their peers. There can be many reasons for this, but it often comes down to one of two things: a lack of individual student agency or interest or unclear expectations and follow-through from the teacher. Understanding where the breakdown happened and then finding a solution for the particular problem is important. The feedback process isn't designed to happen in a vacuum; the challenges that arise can actually strengthen students' learning, collaboration, and leadership skills. In the following section, a student recalls the sometimes messy experience of being editor-in-chief of her high school newspaper.

Three years ago, as a high school senior, I was given the honor of being the editor-in-chief of the *Blazer*. During this vital transition from one stage of my life to a much bigger one, being on the newspaper staff motivated me to have a voice. Not only was I able to improve the precision of my writing, but I also published articles on topics I found interesting, strengthened my ability to give constructive criticism, and learned the value of collaboration.

As editor-in-chief, I had the privilege of forming an everlasting bond with my adviser. The idea was for her to take a hands-off approach to allow student leaders to develop their skills, but without her assistance, I would not have learned how to give good feedback or be a good leader. No one wants to hear that their work is subpar, but there's a gentle and effective approach to addressing ways of improvement. I chose to hold one-on-one meetings as often as possible because I found in-person communication to be more genuine and sensitive. This technique also allowed me to listen to other writers and improved my confidence in actually being heard. It's easier to dismiss a digital comment than one given directly.

As with any team project, creative disagreement sometimes arose. In one instance, a reporter questioned my leadership abilities and ignored my feedback. At first, I was angry with this staff member. I found his opinion audacious, especially because it was never directly expressed to me. Conflict is intimidating. I was unsure how to fix the dissatisfaction in a productive way but felt it my responsibility as a leader to do something. Taking a step back to analyze the situation, I concluded that this was not something I had to do alone and that I shouldn't allow another's words to hurt my confidence in my abilities. My adviser's confidence in me and support during and after the incident encouraged resolution, which we reached after several heartfelt discussions. Although this also meant the resignation of the staff member, moving forward, the remainder of the team and I had more open communication.

Despite my leadership role, I was not the holder of all knowledge. I was a student, just like my peers, and I believe that this conflict showed them that my priority was growth, not power. Teamwork is a leadership skill; it kept me grounded during a time when my ego could easily have become inflated by my position as editor-in-chief.

My role as a leader did not come to an end when I walked across the stage at graduation. Now nearing the end of my junior year of college, I have held a Resident Assistant position for three semesters and will be returning as an RA next year. This role requires leadership, collaborative, and organizational skills and entails conflict and time management, completion of administrative tasks, and more. During my initial interview, I was asked to discuss a time when I resolved a team conflict, and I passionately explained the above instance. I may not have earned the position solely because of my background in collaboration and conflict resolution, but I definitely would not be where I am today without my experience at the *Blazer*.

Academically, I have been complimented on my writing style. Professors have commented on my "effective rule breaking," and I believe this stems from needing to be concise as a journalist. I've been unafraid to approach professors with questions about their comments in large part because of the practice the newspaper provided. In addition, I feel confident in participating in peer review because the process truly does enhance the end piece. Feedback doesn't necessarily have to be a scary thing. It can be given with the best intentions and creates a great opportunity for growth.

—*Deborah Kosnar*

Deborah's story is not an uncommon one. When teachers allow students to resolve conflicts and take control of situations, they grow in ways both intended and unintended, making the classroom a richer, more meaningful place to learn. To create such a dynamic learning space, however, the classroom must provide a safe, supportive culture in which students feel free to take risks and fail—a topic explored in Chapter 2.

Reflection Questions

1. What changes would you need to make to allow students to take the necessary risks in your class?

2. What are some unintended consequences of growth, and how can you build on them in the future?

3. If you're not seeing student leadership emerging in your classes, what are the biggest roadblocks?

2

DEVELOPING A
SUPPORTIVE
CLASSROOM
CULTURE

Incorporating peer feedback into your classroom isn't as simple as saying, "Today, we are going to give each other feedback." A classroom is like a playground for learning: if we want kids to play nicely, we have to develop a welcoming, respectful learning environment that supports risk taking and honest sharing. Students must first feel comfortable enough to share their work and then gain confidence to provide feedback to others. For deeper learning to happen, every choice we make should support the dynamic we seek to nurture.

This chapter explores how to create an environment of mutual respect and support—by building rapport and respect, establishing rituals and routines, celebrating success and failure, and letting students take the lead—and shares real-life examples of what student-led learning environments look like.

Building Rapport and Respect

At the beginning of the year, make it a priority to develop a rapport with students by finding out about their outside interests and offering opportunities for them to share what matters to them. Developing a rapport also means giving yourself the chance to be more human to students. You can start by sharing things about your own school experiences or family. There's no need to open up beyond your comfort zone, but when students see us as whole people, they are more inclined to open up to us and one another.

Developing a respectful classroom culture is not as easy as the warm and fuzzy sharing of experiences, although that is a fine start. Teachers need to safeguard student pride and ensure that the classroom is as free of negative judgment as possible. It isn't acceptable for students to say nasty things to one another or make fun of something they don't understand. It takes vigilance to make sure that all voices are being heard and respected in all classroom activities and situations. Respect can't be assumed; it must be taught explicitly and modeled continuously. Because students tend to follow our lead, the best way to elicit high-quality, respectful feedback is to start modeling these behaviors from day one. If we want students to respect one another, we in turn should be respectful when speaking to students, handling conflicts, and addressing multiple perspectives. Some ideas for getting started include

• Holding open forums to invite student voices and suggestions on all kinds of topics and issues that affect the learning environment, ranging from classroom management to project feedback to grouping. Students can share ideas in a class discussion or meeting, contribute comments anonymously, or offer suggestions privately for the teacher to relay to the whole class. Twitter is also a great platform that enables reticent students to share freely.

• Administering surveys that elicit feedback about classroom learning. After reviewing the survey results, you can share outcomes and adjust your pedagogy accordingly. Figure 2.1 shows an example of a class survey. Some questions I have asked include

- What topics covered did you find most useful?
- Which assignment did you find most useful and why?
- Which assignment did you find least useful and why?
- What would you have liked to spend more time on?
- How did you feel about the reading selection?
- Do you believe the pace and scope of the class are appropriate?
- What skills do you think you have mastered in this class?
- Do you think you were given enough conferencing time to get your individual needs met?
- This year, we did in-class conferences using Google Forms to prepare you and track your own learning. How helpful was this process?
- What advice would you give me for teaching this class in the future?

- Engaging in fishbowl activities that have students role-play situations that call for feedback, such as conferences or group work, in front of their classmates, and then discuss the skits as a class. Students will see how to handle a variety of feedback scenarios and build a respectful learning culture.

Figure 2.1 | Sample Class Survey and Results

AP Lit Class Evaluation Form

This is a teacher feedback from. Your honesty and thoughts are deeply appreciated. Nothing will be held against you. I'm merely using this as a way to improve the course. Thanks in advance for your feedback.

What topics covered did you find most useful?

Please select as many or as few as apply.

☐ Poetry unit

☐ *Animal Farm*—author's craft at work

☐ Satire—"A Modest Proposal"

☐ Satire—*Gulliver's Travels*

☐ *Great Expectations*—coming-of-age novels written in serial

☐ How to write a lit analysis paper

☐ *The Great Gatsby*—the great American novel

☐ *Pride and Prejudice*—historical portrayals

☐ *Hamlet*—Shakespearean tragedy

☐ *Rosencrantz and Guildenstern Are Dead*—absurdist theater

☐ Research paper

☐ Literature blogs

☐ Other: _____

Continued on next page

Figure 2.1 | Sample Class Survey and Results—(continued)

Results of Topic Survey

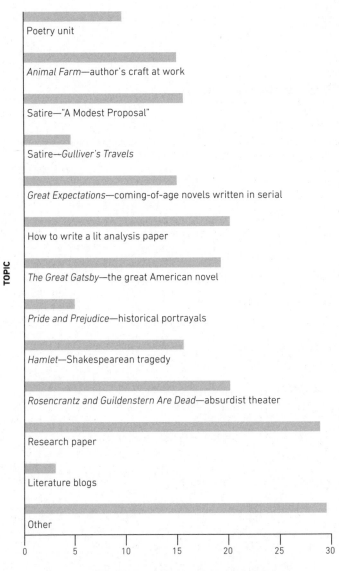

NUMBER OF STUDENTS WHO FOUND TOPIC USEFUL

Figure 2.1 | Sample Class Survey and Results—(continued)

Assignment Survey with Two Student Responses			
Which assignment did you find least useful and why?	What would you have liked to spend more time on?	How did you feel about the reading selection?	Do you feel the pace and scope of the class are appropriate?
The CPAS I found least useful because of its redundancy. We had already discussed and practiced the things that it asked us to do, so it was pointless to me.	I would have liked to spend more time on the AP test preparation. That week for the exam I felt was a little too rushed and could have been stretched out more over the course of the year.	I really liked the reading selection, it was classical and consisted of books that everyone talks about and that we would need to know about for college. I would have liked something completely random and original, like a not-well-known science fiction book or something, to create more of a variety.	I found them to be very appropriate, yes. At first the timing of the reaction papers scared me because of everything else, but once I got the hang of it, I found it to be one of the easiest assignments of all my classes.
The assignment I found least useful was the CPAS. Maybe it was just me, but I felt very uninspired and stuck while doing it. The whole satire unit in general was not fun or educational for me. To be totally honest I hated it.	I think I would've liked to spend more time on novels that were written in the 20th century rather than the 19th century, *Animal Farm* in particular. That unit seemed very quick, and I would've liked to analyze the novel a bit more because it's one that actually interested me, while *Gulliver's Travels, Great Expectations*, and *Pride and Prejudice* all bored me and I will probably never pick them up again.	I understand that *Great Expectations* was a coming-of-age novel and unit, but it would've been so much better if we'd read *Catcher in the Rye* instead. Now that's the ultimate coming-of-age novel of all time, and it would've been great analyzing it in class.	I was expecting a lot of work from this class and I definitely got it. I feel the pace was actually perfect. We weren't bombarded with work, and if we ever felt overwhelmed, the feeling of accomplishing all of the work in the end was worth the turmoil of getting it all done in time.

Establishing Rituals and Routines

Rituals and routines are essential to developing rapport and expectations in a learning environment. Consistency is necessary for students to gain trust; the worst choice a teacher can make is to be too flexible at the beginning of the year and never establish clear expectations. The way classroom routines are established may vary depending on students' age and level, but the idea behind them will not: students need to understand how and why things are happening, and they need to be invested in the systems in place.

Note that consistency doesn't mean stagnancy. Rituals and routines should be adjusted as students grow throughout the year, using appropriate protocols that ensure that every student's needs are being met. Eventually, students can help create and reinforce rituals and routines. For example, say you establish a class discussion protocol at the beginning of the year in which you ask a question and model the expectation, give students time to write, and then have students discuss the question in small groups or pairs before bringing it to the whole group. This protocol makes it possible for all students to talk to at least one person about his or her ideas, but it is still somewhat teacher-led. Later in the year, you might decide to hand off class discussions to students by allowing them to develop their own questions (individually, in small groups, or as a whole class) and then use the same protocol to follow their own inquiry. In this setting, you can facilitate rather than lead the conversation.

Celebrating Success *and* Failure

Every student comes to the table with a variety of strengths and challenges. For real learning to happen, failure must not be feared but embraced. If we take the time to reframe failure as opportunity, then students will feel free to take the big risks that can accelerate progress. I suggest instituting routines in your class that celebrate both success and failure and nudge students to push themselves beyond what they already do well. Here are some ways in which you can encourage failing forward and create a safe atmosphere for learning:

• Offer opportunities for students to share the most wrong answers. No, that's not a typo! If class discussion seems stifled, break the ice by asking students to give an answer that they know is incorrect. This exercise gets students thinking about the content, encourages them to think outside the box, and loosens them up for discussion. Because the aim is to guess wrong answers, students who are usually afraid to contribute will feel more comfortable participating in class. You can easily use these wrong answers to eventually lead the discussion to the right answers, and in the meantime you'll have created an atmosphere where students feel that being wrong is OK—even celebrated. Younger students tend to be more immediately comfortable with this exercise, but high school students love it, too.

• Rather than have students raise their hands to speak, have them throw a soft ball or toy around to determine who has the floor. Ask students to call on one another and, rather than worry about being right or wrong, to build on what other students have said.

• Teach and model giving warm and cool feedback on student work: first recognizing a strength and then posing a question or an idea that prompts the receiver to think about the content from a different perspective. Anonymity may be appropriate the first few times, but after that students should be encouraged to take ownership of their words and feedback.

• At the end of each unit, celebrate any missteps and connect them directly to the positive growth that emerged from them to help students see that initial failures or mistakes are what led to their eventual success.

• Share stories regularly about mistakes you have made and how and why you were able to succeed after the failure. For example, one year I had a great idea to conduct a tea party socializing experiment around *Pride and Prejudice*. But I hadn't thought it through enough, and when it came time to actually do it, it didn't go very well. So I stopped class in the middle, brainstormed with the students on ideas for improvement, and called for a do-over the next day. With the ideas we came up with and the extra preparation, the tea party was a bigger success on the second day, and every student was more invested and engaged.

In addition to celebrating failure, be sure to recognize positive growth both privately and publicly. It's important to find time to rejoice in students' progress, giving these moments as much priority as those focused on improvement and letting students know that you know they are growing. Sometimes students feel stagnant in their learning and aren't progressing as quickly as they'd like. All it takes is one person noticing and acknowledging growth for struggling students to see it, too.

Here are some thoughts from a former student on learning to embrace peer feedback—successes, failures, and all.

Feedback is one of the most significant parts of the writing process; if done right, it can make a difference in how students improve and value their work. However, often feedback is unappreciated and feared, as students perceive it as a criticism of their paper as well as of their writing skills.

The first time I received feedback from another student was in my newspaper class. The editor, although successful at highlighting the good and bad aspects of my article, seemed cold and highly critical. This was discouraging and eventually led to a fear of opening my article, knowing that it would be highlighted by yellow sticky notes all over the place, making me feel like everything was wrong. It was not until later that year, when I began to peer-review other students' papers, that I realized how beneficial and encouraging feedback can be.

My transition from fearing feedback to enjoying it did not happen overnight. When I first began to comment on other students' papers, I was concerned with how I would sound. I wanted to make sure that my suggestions not only were helpful but also maintained a tone that was positive and supportive. I decided that the best way to do this was to give a balance of comments that highlighted strengths and weakness, along with an explanation for each. I also made sure to include suggestions or examples for how to fix certain issues. This allowed the students to understand why they got the feedback and how the corrections could be made. Once I got into the habit of following this method, I started to become more confident in my ability to provide effective and positive feedback.

In newspaper, the feedback process helped me learn the guidelines, which eventually allowed my work to become an example for my peers of what a good article should and should not include. As a writer, receiving feedback not only improved my papers every time but also made me appreciate the feedback. All of this came with the mindset: "Even if the peer reviews seem negative, my work is good, but it has the potential to be better."

Now I actually enjoy getting feedback for my writing, especially from someone who does not know me, because as a writer it is important to be critical of your work and acknowledge the parts that need improvement. After a while, I was able to begin to notice what I was doing wrong and fix it on my own. This elevated my writing, and as I mastered one skill, I was able to learn and develop new ones.

The fact is that writing is a self-taught revolutionary process. There are various levels of writing, and no writer is perfect. We all go through the same process: beginning with an outline, then writing the first draft, revising, asking for feedback, revising some more, and at last completing the final product. Being open to this process is essential and can lead to more confidence in one's work.

Letting Students Take the Lead

The student-led classroom is probably not what you or your parents remember about school. It's noisy and chaotic at times, but filled with an air of possibility that you don't find in classrooms where the teacher is hyperfocused on intended outcomes. When students lead, learning always happens, whether it's knowledge acquisition or development of life skills and transferrable mastery skills.

One hallmark of the student-led classroom is students' clear autonomy and ownership of their learning. Kids retain the rights to their beliefs and thoughts about what they read and hear, while their teachers prompt them to deepen and support their assertions with evidence and critical thinking. Teachers don't necessarily have to agree with a student to support a line of inquiry; our job is to be open-minded and encourage students to follow a path that leads the exploration forward.

Challenges may arise for teachers who are just starting out with this approach and for seasoned teachers alike. Ceding control of a class's learning can be messy. Here are some do's and don'ts to make the transition smoother and more effective:

- *Don't* go in with lingering reservations. It will soon be clear if you're merely paying lip service to the idea of a student-led classroom, claiming to give students ownership of their learning without really embracing the idea.
- *Do* remain actively involved on the back end, gathering data and making adjustments as needed.
- *Don't* give students control before you've put the proper rituals and routines in place.
- *Do* be transparent about expectations. Define students' roles and remain engaged as a facilitator. Without your guidance, students can learn quickly how to get around expectations, at a cost to their learning.
- *Do* continually take the "temperature" of the class and engage in on-the-spot feedback. This is a good way to model the behavior for students.

Management-related and similar issues in a student-led classroom aren't unlike those in a traditional classroom. It's important to strike a balance between being vigilant and allowing students to do their own thing. Expect some days to be better than others, and don't give up. The benefits are worth any growing pains you and your students experience at the outset. Once students adjust to the new dynamic, they tend to engage more fully in their learning, too. Here are some student insights about student-led classrooms:

In a student-led classroom, students are not as intimidated, because the person teaching the class is their age. Sometimes, a strong and understanding connection between a student and a teacher is essential for learning, and if the teacher is the same age and has the same mindset, then it can be easier to teach. The student teaching may have more effective methods as well, given they understand better how the students' minds work. I also feel like students pay more attention, because it isn't "just some boring adult talking and lecturing." A challenge can be that the student leading may not speak or provide information as well as a teacher, given they did not go through the training of teaching. Having knowledge doesn't necessarily mean they can teach it.

Student-led classrooms are different from what we are normally accustomed to. A great percentage of people picture a classroom setting as a teacher standing in front of students, teaching the content to the students. However, in a student-led classroom, the teacher does not give lectures. In Ms. Sackstein's newspaper class, she makes any announcements she has. Then, she checks up on our progress to make sure we are on task. Everything else is in the hands of the students. Although Ms. Sackstein does check up on us, she is not the one to e-mail students to get their work in on time. Student leaders e-mail the rest of the students to check up on their progress. When we come across uncertain rules as we write articles, we ask our editors. If the editors aren't sure, then we ask Ms. Sackstein. We do not ask her immediately. Compared with the stereotypical classroom, there are a lot more student interactions in student-led classrooms. I feel like this learning environment builds teamwork and develops the ability to find one's own solutions.

—Kahyun Kim

A Look Inside Student-Led Classrooms

My newspaper class provides a powerful example of a student-led classroom culture. Students control what and how they learn almost from the beginning of the year. Student editors, who serve as class leaders, are trained to provide excellent feedback to staffers as well as to me to ensure that our website is functioning like a professional online media outlet.

To ensure a smooth transition of leadership from year to year as well as build confidence in the following year's staff, each year the 12th grade student editors recommend certain 11th grade reporters who show promise in particular areas. Once I give the go-ahead, the senior editors notify these reporters and discuss the possibility of their becoming editors the following year. We then go through a vetting process that involves setting up meetings and training the juniors who are interested. Apprenticing under the senior editors, they work as assistants, with the seniors checking their work and providing additional feedback as they go. Students know what they're supposed to be doing because they have clear routines to follow. On any given day, the room will look different according to the needs of those in the room.

My journalism classroom isn't the only one that empowers students in this way, of course. In the following section, a colleague shares an example of student empowerment in her classroom.

In the journalism classroom, we cannot grow or improve without feedback and critique. Although we want to foster a supportive environment for peer feedback, we know that pointing out mistakes can be misconstrued. Therefore, the tutorial model of peer-guided inquiry (see below) guides the learner along the path to discovering the answer rather than just telling the learner what he or she did wrong.

Yearbook Design Tutorial—Publications

Objective: How does understanding the rules of modular design help shape an effective yearbook spread?

Preparation for Tutorial

1. Print your spread.
2. Write down what you know is correct on your spread (use rubric for talking points). *I know…*
3. Write down what you still have questions about regarding your spread design. *I'm wondering…*

Tutorial Day
Each designer presents his or her spread. First, explain what you already know you've done well on your spread. Next, discuss which areas you are seeking input on. The tutorial audience will help guide you toward improving your spread by asking guiding questions *only*. The audience should not simply *tell* presenters what to change but remind the presenters of their learning and offer suggestions via questioning. Audience members and presenters will take notes. Repeat until all designers have presented.

Sample guiding questions from the audience:

- Can you tell us more about why you chose that photo as the dominant image?
- Do you remember what we learned about using contrast in design (e.g., headline)?
- What are the visual theme elements? How have you incorporated them?
- What are the verbal theme elements? How have you incorporated them?

- Did you choose the best photos for your spread?
- Have you chosen a variety of shots covering many students using the 1, 2, 3+ rule?
- Do all of your captions follow the caption format?
- Can you show me the eyeline on your design?
- Do you remember what we learned about pica spacing? How did you use it with your grouped photos?

Reflection: What is one question that was discussed today that will help you improve your spread? How did today's tutorial help refine your vision for your spread?

The setup of a tutorial has the student presenter first establish what he or she knows is correct about his or her work (perhaps using a rubric for guidance). Then the student identifies a "point of confusion" or a list of questions that he or she still has about his or her work. In this case, it would be questions about how to improve his or her yearbook spread, but this model could also apply to writing or any subject area across the curriculum.

Once the presenter has explained what was done well and raised the point of confusion, it is up to the supportive peer audience to use questions to guide the presenter to see how to improve. For the first time or two, it might be necessary to model the inquiry process by giving the audience a few example questions. As students become more comfortable with the process and the content, they should be able to formulate the questions on their own.

During the process, the presenter and the audience should be taking notes on the interactions, both to record the thought process and to guide their learning. At the end of the process, student presenters should reflect on what question or questions from the audience helped them improve most. They can also comment on how the tutorial process fostered their own discovery of learning in a way that just being told what was wrong and how to fix it wouldn't.

This tutorial model creates a positive and supportive peer feedback environment because everyone has questions, and everyone is there to help the presenters improve. This model can be adapted to all content areas and to diverse assignments that range in complexity. At the heart of the model are student discovery and a positive model for inquiry and collaboration.

—Rachel Rauch

The lifeblood of a student-centered classroom is inquiry, and allowing students to have control over where the questions go is essential. Maintaining a space where we value students' processes and empower them to share what they know is important. The tutorial model above has students take notes during the tutorials and make explicit connections to how this process informs their own inquiry moving forward. Forming these connections helps the audience members to learn from the work of their classmates.

Empowering students to lead their own learning needn't be limited to high school classrooms; elementary school students, too, can benefit from a student-led model. Let's take, for example, Doug Robertson's 5th graders. Doug, who has written a book and maintains a blog titled *He's the Weird Teacher* (http://hestheweirdteacher.blogspot.com), lets his students sit where they like and question the material in a way that offers them freedom. In the following section, Doug elaborates on the thinking behind providing such an environment as well as the positive results it yields.

My classroom has a lot of seating options. That may not sound important, but I believe that all aspects of a classroom play into all other aspects. I'm interested in creating a space where students feel free to take control of their learning. What message does it send when I start with not letting them control their seating? "You should be able to guide your own thinking, but I'm telling you how to sit in a chair." I've got bean bag chairs, foam cubes, wobble stools, and more. I've got standing desks and traditional desks and desks that sit right on the floor. Every day students switch chairs and I'm willing to change the height of their desks when they ask. This creates an atmosphere of control and empowerment. You choose the body position that your body tells you works best today.

It's a start to a much more pervasive message.

I spend a lot of time telling my 5th graders, "That's a really good question."

Then I walk away. And that's where their learning almost starts.

I don't walk directly away and never talk to them again. That's not how teaching works. That develops no culture of trust. Often I'll cough, "Dictionary!" I'll dramatically intone while lying across two desks, "If only, if only we had something somewhere that had the answers you seek!" And I wait. In short order students poke each other and point at the Chromebooks, Macbooks, and iPads scattered about the room. "Can we use a computer?"

"A computer!" I shout. "Genius!"

And that's where the learning nearly starts.

Teaching students to look something up isn't as easy as "Go ask the Google." The Google, you see, has All The Answers. It's not akin to using a magnet to find a needle in a haystack. It's finding a needle in a stack of needles. They need to learn to search in order to learn.

And that's where their learning starts.

My students don't Google everything. What fun is that? Google lives in conjunction with my class directive of Make a Thing. This is where my students truly take charge of their learning.

My class takes charge of their own learning often, and it started early. The first story in our reading text—yes, even student-directed classrooms use the district texts; why throw away a tool when you can bend it to your will instead?—was taken from the delightful book *Sideways Stories from Wayside School* by Louis Sachar. The chapter chosen involved Ms. Jewls, the teacher at the top of the school (Wayside School was built 30 stories tall rather than 30 classrooms long, you see), letting her students throw objects from their window to the playground far below. They are trying to learn about how fast they'll learn.

The entire story is pretty ridiculous, so my class monster posed a challenge to my students through a video. (I have a class monster; his name is Courson. They like him better than they like me, so sometimes he makes videos to tell them about projects.) Courson asked my kids if the book was right. Would a lighter object and a heavier object fall at the same rate? Figure it out and explain why.

Remember how I keep saying, "And that's where the learning starts"? The second half of that directive, that's where the learning really happens. It is not enough that my kids are now standing up, standing on chairs, holding a textbook and a pencil, and dropping them at the same time. That's fun, that they are seeing the practical application of a force of nature is great, but it's not understanding. They test because they want to, and the more they test, the more they see: "Wait, the weight doesn't matter? Paper falls slower, but it's floating, so that's not fair. Ball it up. See? Same as the book. That's weird!"

I want "That's weird." Because then I can step in and say, "So why does it work?" But if I've trained my class correctly and they feel the freedom, they take it upon themselves to think, "That's weird!" and then think, "I wonder why." And go looking. Soon my 5th graders know about gravity as a real force and not just as a Sandra Bullock movie. Their exploration takes them deeper than a lecture or even Bill Nye, whom I love and worship, could have taken them.

—*Doug Robertson*

Students of all ages can be given choices and empowered to take control of their learning. If we want students to remain engaged and thoughtful about their growth, we've got to do everything in our power to make sure that those choices stay in our learners' hands regardless of what grade they are in.

Both Doug and Rachel shared stories about the power of student choice. The more pervasive these concepts are in all classes, the better equipped our students will be in the future to ask the necessary questions and take charge of their own lives. These skills transcend content and grade and can be built into classes every year.

Remember that we can't just ask kids to go do stuff. Learning new material and skills takes a good deal of instruction and practice with feedback weaved in. Why not show them, ask them to show you—and then set them loose?

Reflection Questions

1. Take an honest inventory of where you are in the process of increasing students' control over their learning. Is your classroom a shared space where students' voices matter and contribute to decision making? If so, how does student leadership affect learning? How do you know? If not, how can you give students more power and foster an environment in which student feedback will flourish?

2. Take some time to write about your situation. Don't be afraid to elicit feedback from your students; just make sure to really listen if you ask. Then consider how you can take what you hear and apply it to changing your learning environment.

3

WHAT MEANINGFUL FEEDBACK LOOKS LIKE

Before we can teach students to give one another feedback, we need to gain a deeper understanding of what good feedback is and how it helps learners become more adept at what they are seeking feedback on. When we provide feedback, we're entering into a contract with the learner that we'll first determine what he or she needs and then do the best in our power to deliver the feedback in a way that he or she can understand.

Unfortunately, much so-called feedback consists of empty platitudes: "Nice work!" "Good job!" "Big improvement." Our education culture is full of such nice-sounding phrases that distract from what is too often the truth: we aren't really paying attention. When we say "Excellent!" or "Way to go!" we mean well, but we're not providing anything beyond a momentary ego stroke.

To ensure truly effective and meaningful feedback, you'll need to make sure that several important elements are in place. This chapter discusses how to set the stage for effective feedback with clear learning goals, what the feedback itself should do, and the logistics of creating a feedback-rich environment.

Establishing Clear Learning Goals

Before you even reach the feedback stage, it's important to set everyone up for success by ensuring clear learning goals and criteria for success. Here are some important steps for building a strong foundation for meaningful feedback:

• With each assignment, consider the "work" of learning that you're offering to students. Is it worthy of feedback? What is its purpose? Can you easily answer these questions? Can your students?

• Clearly spell out and communicate learning objectives or learning targets and criteria for success prior to the learning experience, and continually refer to them throughout the formative learning process. You can do this by going over assignment sheets before work has begun on a project or doing activities that prepare students for the expectations of the assessment.

• Use questioning activities and discussion to help students develop their own goals around learning objectives, and explicitly connect them to prior and future learning.

• Consider using annotation protocols that have students highlight and make notes on the assignment sheet and then work in small groups to interview, or question, the expectations of the assessment. For example, students can write a checkmark next to areas that connect to work that has come already, a plus sign next to new skills or ideas, and a question mark next to expectations that seem unclear. They can then develop clarifying questions before beginning the assignment and revisit the annotated assignment as needed throughout the process of completing the assignment, which covers the course of a unit.

• Align learning objectives with the standards and the big picture of the lesson or unit. You can do this by sharing essential questions or a unit plan with students upfront so that they know the scope and sequence at the outset.

• To help students internalize learning, be sure that they understand the language of the learning objectives and standards and that they see the connections between the two. Consider scaffolding the process by asking students questions that get them thinking about what they've already learned both in your class and in others and then asking them to reflect on their prior learning at the beginning of a new project. Allow students to rewrite standards or objectives in words that make sense to them.

• When you introduce a new assignment, spend some time going over exemplars that meet the criteria for success. Mastery shouldn't be a guessing game. If possible, don't use a sample assignment that is identical to the one you are actually giving students; this can inhibit creativity and learning. Have students brainstorm in small groups, and then as a whole class, what mastery looks like.

Providing Good Feedback

Effective feedback is specific, timely, and delivered in a way that works for the receiver. The following tips will help you hone your own feedback and model the process to students.

• Focus on one or two points at a time rather than trying to address everything at once. Keep the feedback tight and focused on specific learning goals. It's even better if students set these goals themselves. Students should share goals with one another so that teachers and peer evaluators are clear on the areas that require feedback.

• Ask students to write about the learning goals they set in a reflection once they finish their work. Review the reflection or conference with students, and then provide feedback on the areas students are working on. For example, if students are working on building context in an introductory paragraph, then highlight successful areas of their writing in clear, specific terms. Rather than "Good job," you might comment, "You've improved on your ability to add context to engage the reader." Figure 3.1 (see p. 40) shows an example of such feedback.

• Provide specific student-friendly strategies. When your feedback is critical, provide strategies or possible solutions for improving the area of need. It's easy enough to say that a transition needs to be smoothed out, but why not offer a little more? "Smooth the transitions between these paragraphs by adding an additional 'foreshadowing' sentence in the paragraph before to prepare the reader for the shift that is about to happen," or "Move beyond simple transitional phrases to ease your reader into the new idea."

• Be specific even when your feedback is positive so that students know what they're doing well. It's good to use the language of whatever success criteria you're working with so the connections can become clearer throughout. For example, "I love the way you interpreted Orwell's purpose through your characterization of Napoleon" or "You clearly understand the necessary steps to solving a quadratic equation as you've taken the time to write it out correctly and add a visual representation. Can I use this as an example to share with one of your peers?"

• Limit your feedback to the material covered. No surprises! Giving students unrelated feedback will not be helpful and may even be counterproductive. For example, if your class is learning about how to use the scientific method when conducting experiments and has only gotten to the point of developing a hypothesis, do not provide feedback on the steps that come after (e.g., analyzing data).

Figure 3.1 | Example of Feedback Specific to Student Learning Goals

Setting Up a Feedback-Rich Environment

We've explored how to set the stage for effective feedback by ensuring clear learning goals as well as what the feedback itself should do. Now let's look at the logistics of setting up an environment conducive to peer as well as teacher feedback.

• The best time to begin offering feedback is during the formative process, preferably after you have taught the skill or content and students have already done some work. Providing feedback too early in the process can be damaging because the person giving the feedback may inadvertently take ownership of the work. For example, parents who "help" their children with homework don't intend to do the whole assignment, but they often end up taking over. Consider pairing students who are having a hard time getting started with classmates who aren't having trouble to bounce ideas off each other in brainstorming conversations. Ensure that the "helper" partner isn't the one recording the ideas; the student who feels stuck should take notes so that he or she can take ownership of his or her ideas.

• Encourage students to track their own progress and then check in regularly so that you can align your expectations with theirs.

• Practice, practice, practice. Giving good feedback is an art form that does require practice, so the more we do it, the better it gets. As we make feedback an integral part of the learning experience, it becomes easier to make smaller, more frequent adjustments for optimal growth.

• Take opportunities to offer informal feedback while students are working. Walk around the room, read over students' shoulders, ask them questions about what you see, and give them feedback on the spot. Students can write down this feedback in a designated spot in their notebooks and apply it to their learning immediately.

• Remember that feedback isn't separate from teaching; the teaching is in the feedback. This is an educator's opportunity to privately share information that fosters growth. Whether we do it in writing, in a face-to-face conference, over a Google Hangout, or on a Voxer, each time we share ideas about what we see based on a specific success criterion or standard, we are offering learners another opportunity to hear where they stand, adjust and practice, and move forward. A side benefit is that these moments help us develop deeper relationships with our students, which increases their investment in learning.

A Note on Weak or Nonconstructive Feedback

As I mentioned at the beginning of this chapter, vague positive feedback doesn't help students grow. Neither does nonstrategic critical feedback. Try to avoid making critical comments when there's no larger constructive goal behind them. Even feedback perceived as critical can result in an erosion of the student-teacher rapport that can be extremely difficult to overcome. Rebuilding lost trust is a burden you don't need to add to your workload. To avoid finding yourself in this situation and continuously improve the feedback process, I suggest modeling and teaching active listening strategies, including

- Making direct eye contact when you deliver feedback.
- Concentrating on only one task at a time (in this instance, listening).
- Repeating back what you hear verbatim before continuing to ensure you've understood the other person correctly.
- Using a sentence starter like "I heard you say...."
- Using a sentence construction like "When you said..., I was wondering/I was unclear about...."
- Observing and following the other's nonverbal cues. Notice his or her response to your feedback, as shown in facial expression and posture, for example, and adjust your tone accordingly.

Always be mindful of the tone in which you share critical feedback. If you have a lot to share, make sure you do it in person, or at least not solely in writing. When you spend so much time developing a climate of comfort and learning, one misstep can impair the learning process. However, we all make mistakes, so it is essential to recover and model corrective behaviors as quickly as possible. If you see a student shutting down while you're sharing feedback, stop. Now is not the right time to continue. Instead, say something encouraging and revisit the issue at a later time, when the student is more receptive. Teaching students to be receptive to feedback is an important topic we'll explore in Chapter 4.

Reflection Questions

1. How do you currently provide feedback to your students? How often do you allow students to provide feedback to you?

2. Consider a time when you received useful feedback. What about it made it useful, and how did you grow from it? What can you take from that experience and apply to the feedback you provide to others?

PART 2

INTRODUCING STUDENTS TO FEEDBACK

4

TEACHING STUDENTS TO RECEIVE AND APPLY FEEDBACK

There are certain skills that we expect to be innate or that we don't bother teaching because we assume students have picked them up at some point. Receiving and applying feedback appropriately involves two such skills that we can and should teach students: (1) the ability to receive critical feedback and (2) the ability to understand how to grow from that feedback. This chapter will help you teach these two essential skills to students by helping them accept feedback, developing their listening skills, and teaching them to apply feedback to their learning.

Teaching Students to Receive Feedback

Here's what two 11th graders had to say about how peer feedback has influenced their learning:

One way the process of peer feedback helps is that you learn good lessons from your peers. I've learned from other editors lessons such as leaving out opinions for the betterment of the piece or learning how to phrase an opinion objectively.

Your peers are often easier to talk to than a teacher, and it is helpful to hear perspectives of your intended audience. Through peer feedback, I get many opinions and see how others perceive my work. Since I am writing for a specific age group, it's very useful to see what they think. I received a lot of beneficial tips for writing news pieces, and I learned a variety of techniques from other students. Tools that help them in making their writing substantial are shared with me.

These two students have reaped the benefits of peer feedback, but they probably weren't thrilled to get critical feedback at first. Getting to the point of accepting feedback from peers can be a rough road. Hearing critical feedback, in particular, isn't pleasant. Sure, in the long term it will help students grow as learners, but it can be challenging to get past disappointment or a bruised ego, especially for younger or less mature students. This section explores ways to help students become more receptive to critical feedback as well as develop their listening skills.

Helping Reluctant Learners Accept Feedback

You'll find that some students eat up feedback—positive, negative, or neutral—and will eagerly make requested corrections and resubmit their work within minutes. On the whole, these are the easy students to deal with; they want to learn, and they recognize that the process requires a thick skin and plenty of perseverance. The challenge with some of these students is teaching them to be more independent because they crave continuous feedback and attention.

The students who generate the most amount of work are those who don't (or won't) recognize that their work isn't up to par and don't want to hear that it needs improvement. These students' misconceptions about their learning are problematic but not insurmountable. It's especially important to address these challenges head-on to ensure that students are open when it comes time to receive peer feedback.

If you've created a supportive classroom culture and built relationships with your students, you'll know who these students are already. Last year I had a 12th grade student who thought his work was better than it really was. He wrote reflection after reflection suggesting that he was meeting or exceeding standards when I knew he wasn't. He was never available for the extra help or meetings I offered, but he would regularly send me an urgent plea for help via Voxer the night before a long-term project or paper was due. Unfortunately, he always left it so late that there was never much I could do to help.

We worked all year on his time management skills, since beginning his projects earlier would give him an idea of what kind of assistance he'd need, but he didn't want to make the effort to change his work habits. So we had to work with what we had. Here are some ways I was able to help him become more receptive to feedback:

- I asked him to reach out via Voxer or invite me to his Google Doc well before the project was due so that I could provide specific feedback in small increments. He always heard feedback better when it was delivered in one or two pieces at a time rather than all at once.

- We went through pieces of his work together during class time. I asked him to highlight areas he felt he needed help in and focused on teaching him to articulate skills from the current work and then compare it with other work he had done in the past.

- In class, I'd ask him to work with folks who weren't in his immediate friends circle. At first, I recommended students who could help him. He actually seemed to hear feedback better from his peers than from me.

- When he began showing improvement, I gave him specific feedback on his final drafts that showed him areas of growth. Highlighting parts of the document and using language from the standards and success criteria helped him internalize his goals and see how well he was reaching them. By the end of the year, when we had our final grading conference, he was able to articulate areas of growth and realistically talk about what standards he had met.

Every student is different, so it's important to determine the way each learns best and customize feedback accordingly. Note that the strategies I developed to help my student met him where he was. Make sure to use language that is supportive but honest, and always tie feedback to specific elements of learning. Try to avoid talking about work habits or attitude. It's a given that students who have a hard time hearing critical feedback have other challenges as well, but focusing on skills and content from the learning objectives makes it simpler because they can be discussed with a degree of objectivity. By contrast, addressing attitude or work habits may seem to call students' character into question and thus trigger their defenses. Here are some more things to avoid when trying to help a student be more receptive to feedback:

• **Sarcasm.** This may seem like a no-brainer, but it's important to remember to avoid sarcasm and harsh tones in general. Sarcasm will shut down some students. Make sure your tone is supportive and clear; don't mince words, but don't be harsh.

• **False praise.** Although we want students to feel good about learning, providing them with praise that isn't earned doesn't actually help them. Instead, it softens a blow that they actually need to feel in order to improve, and it dilutes praise to the point that genuine positive feedback won't mean much to them. Use praise only when it's meaningful and deserved.

• **Feedback overload.** Keep your feedback short and simple and address only one or two issues at a time to give learners time and space to digest what they are hearing. Getting all the feedback at once can be overwhelming, and students may shut down or give up in the face of seemingly insurmountable obstacles.

Teachers can foster the grit students need to accept feedback by modeling it. For example, I always tell my students that I am a bad planner when it comes to writing. I often used to skip the outline stage because I thought it took too much time. But my writing suffered for it; I often took too long to get to the point, and my discussion wasn't succinct enough. I realized this after receiving feedback from teachers and peers and began taking the extra time to plan and adjust my writing accordingly. By listening to feedback, I was able to improve. Students are always interested to hear that their writing teacher still needs feedback. When we acknowledge our own mistakes or learning curves in front of students, we are showing them that everyone is on the same journey to improvement and that we all need constructive criticism to grow.

Developing Students' Listening Skills

Much of our ability to receive feedback is tied to our ability to listen well and truly hear what is being said. Again, it may be easy enough to assume that listening is an automatic or innate skill, but that isn't necessarily so. Fortunately, there are things we can do in the classroom to help students really take in what they hear and then be able to use it more appropriately.

Much of what we hear has to do with the speaker's tone, so it's important for students to be able to "read" the tone of whoever is providing feedback. As discussed in Chapter 3, you can use and teach students to use active listening strategies, but you can also take advantage of auditory opportunities to improve students' listening skills prior to hearing feedback.

For example, you can start by playing short podcasts or other "auditory texts" that relate to the lesson, participating as a listener alongside your students. Using a think-aloud protocol, model how you take notes and share what you are thinking while the podcast is running, pausing it as needed. Always make sure at the beginning that students know what to listen for; setting a purpose for listening helps focus students and informs them of where they should take notes or ask clarifying questions. For example, if students in a government class are listening to U.S. senators debate a particular issue that relates to their current topic of study, they can specifically listen for that content. When they prepare for the discussion, they can refer to the auditory text, which sets the stage for future learning while connecting to prior lessons.

After listening to an auditory text, present a short lecture relating back to what they listened to and then let students synthesize what they took away from the text and the lecture. After students have had independent time to reflect, you can move them into small groups, where they can share what they thought were the most important points in the podcast. Then, as a whole class, explore what important information some students may have missed and figure out why. Or students can work independently to generate lists of important points from the auditory text and then provide feedback to one another on their notes, again exploring what was missing from the notes and why, and how they can find that information moving forward.

Repetition is also useful when teaching listening skills because most people need to hear new information more than once to fully absorb it. When you or students are giving important feedback, consider recording it in some way so that the receiver can refer back to it as needed. You can record it in writing, as a comment on a Google Doc, or through tools like Voxer, iMovie, or Screencast-O-Matic.

Remember that students need to practice listening like every other skill, so give them plenty of opportunities. If feasible, you can even use the flipped classroom model and have students watch short videos at home to help improve auditory learning in all content areas.

Teaching Students to Use Feedback to Improve Learning

Once we can be sure that students have heard what we need to tell them, they need to learn to apply it to future learning and skill building. This section includes a scenario from my own classroom to illustrate how the continuous cycle of giving and using feedback works in the classroom as well as strategies to ensure that students are really "getting" the feedback and applying it to their learning.

Helping Students Apply Feedback: A Classroom Scenario

If we've done our job well, students shouldn't just know what they are doing well and what needs work; they will also have strategies to apply in specific areas of need. You can provide these strategies in a number of ways: by commenting on a Google Doc, offering a tip in a one-to-one conference, sharing and prompting ideas in a small group of students who all have the same challenge, or, when most students are struggling with the same skill or content, walking the entire class through strategies.

Last year, it took me three different tries to teach the difference between *summary* and *analysis* before the whole class got it. After reading students' poetry analysis papers (the first in a series of analysis papers they would write), I realized that most students were merely summarizing the information they took from the literature rather than adding value to the evidence they quoted; as far as they were concerned, *analysis* meant *detailed summary* or *explanation*. I knew I needed to slow down and be more intentional: instead of just assuming students knew how to analyze, I needed to explicitly teach them how. It was time for a whole-class lesson that took a different approach from the first one.

I started by posting chart paper on the wall and then asked students to provide me with a quotation from the text (Robert Frost's poem "The Lockless Door") to support the thesis. We used the quotation "It went many years,/But at last came a knock,/And I thought of the door/With no lock to lock" to support the thesis "Throughout 'The Lockless Door,' Robert Frost uses symbolism and repetition to convey the idea that as humans, we are constantly trying to escape the inevitable."

Supporting this assertion calls for more than a cursory understanding of the lines; true analysis requires deeper digging into the specific words and literary devices Frost uses. During the first round of the lesson, I led a think-aloud activity in which I brainstormed what I needed to show to support the thesis, recording my thoughts on the chart paper. Then I wrote the quote on another piece of chart paper that hung next to it and analyzed how Frost's words supported the thesis. Rather than just repeat what the quote was saying by leading in with a similar phrase, I discussed the point I was making, inserted the evidence, and continued to tie my analysis of the evidence back to the thesis, reminding students that their papers should include at least twice as much original writing as text taken from the source.

After this activity, I asked students to do something similar with their table groups. Each group member would write his or her own paragraph analyzing the quotation that I had just used in the class activity. Then the group would pick one in-progress paper to review, offer feedback on, and revise as a team. The students would highlight areas where the analysis was focused and detailed, ensure that it made firm assertions about ideas, and take out wishy-washy wording like "the author seems" or anything that detracted from the certainty of the paper's statements. Once the small groups were able to come up with one good sample analysis, they shared out what they had learned to the class. Finally, students worked independently to revise their own papers using what they had learned.

At the end of the period, I asked students to share their rewritten paragraphs with someone at a different table. Key pieces they were to look for included a clear topic sentence that introduced the new idea, evidence from the text supporting the new idea, the analysis that tied it all back to support the thesis, and a final transition to introduce the next piece of evidence.

When students finished their papers, I asked them to reflect on the process of practicing as a whole class, in small groups, and independently. As I read their reflections, I gained a better understanding of how to teach students the important skill of analysis and was able to establish which students had been able to apply the initial feedback from their drafts and in-class lessons and which students needed further support or alternative strategies.

Ensuring Students Are Getting It

Depending on the subject area and age you teach, along with students' individual needs, you will probably need to differentiate the way you teach students to apply feedback. Here are some strategies to make sure your students are really understanding the feedback they receive and successfully applying it to their learning:

• For younger kids as well as older students with focus-related or organizational challenges, you may want to break up assignment tasks into one part at a time, offering them more opportunities to practice before applying the feedback.

• Ask students to review the feedback provided and, either in person or on the document, to summarize the feedback in their own words and make note of any questions they have. Asking students to summarize will show you how well they understand the feedback, which helps you ensure that they're applying it appropriately to their work. Seeing a student's questions will help you and the student to better articulate the feedback being shared as well as the strategies. It doesn't matter how clearly you believe you are communicating if the student isn't getting it. What matters is what the student actually takes away.

• Before providing new strategies, ask students to think of a strategy they have already learned that they may be able to use to apply the feedback. This connecting activity explicitly demonstrates how skills transfer across contexts and helps students develop mastery in different classes and content areas. For example, a student who has learned to write a thesis statement in English class can apply that knowledge to a document-based question essay in social studies or a hypothesis statement in a lab report. In the beginning, help students make the connections, and remove the training wheels as time goes on.

• Encourage students to find resources on their own and then share the helpful ones with the class. You can reserve a spot on the class website to house a library of resources. It's even better if they are student-made: you may want to ask students to make five-minute tutorial videos on particular content, skills, or tools they know well to aid in future strategy sharing.

• Recruit more advanced students as peer leaders to help you with the process of providing and applying feedback, and encourage students to talk to one another about feedback or confer with a peer leader in a particular area before seeking your help. Whom you pick as peer leaders will vary according to the skills or content you're teaching. Recruiting peer leaders empowers students to use their strengths to help others and demonstrates their mastery to you. It also frees you up to work with students who need more support than a peer can provide.

In my newspaper classes, student editors are the ones who transmit important feedback and improvement strategies to student reporters. I review the feedback provided, dipping into documents periodically and making sure that the reporters understand the feedback provided and know how to use it. Because the peer leaders are doing the initial work, I'm freed up to work one-on-one with students to make sure they know how to move forward. Reporters send their revisions back to the student editors, who review them and then pass them along to the fact checkers and the editor-in-chief, who is responsible for determining when an article is ready to post.

I provided this glimpse into my school newspaper class to illustrate that feedback and revision are an ongoing process. It's important to continually remind students of this fact. Keep this in mind as we move on to Chapter 5, which explains how to introduce students to the feedback process.

Reflection Questions

1. How do you currently teach students to listen and respond to critical feedback?

2. How are you currently teaching students to apply feedback? What kinds of protocols might you implement to make it a part of the learning process in your classes?

5

HELPING STUDENTS UNDERSTAND THE FEEDBACK PROCESS

We've explored why peer feedback is so important, how to create the conditions for it, what meaningful feedback looks like, and how to teach students to receive and apply it. Now it's time to prepare students to use peer feedback in the classroom. This chapter discusses a two-step approach: first helping students to develop and use success criteria and then introducing them to the peer feedback process.

Helping Students Develop and Use Success Criteria

Before students are ready to give, receive, and apply peer feedback, they need to know how to review the work and what to measure it against—in other words, they need to have an idea of what success on the given assignment looks like. Success shouldn't be an amorphous idea, clear only to the teacher. It should be transparent and recognizable, particularly to those who are trying to demonstrate it. This section will help you guide students toward understanding, developing, and using criteria for success by becoming acquainted with students' strengths and challenges and working with them to develop rubrics.

Know the Strengths and Challenges of Your Learners

By the time setting up expert groups (see Chapter 6) is a possibility —approximately two months into the school year—you should have a good idea of your students' strengths and challenges. Here are some ways to facilitate the process in those early weeks:

• While gathering data from the first month or so, record trends and look at the status of the class regularly. Monitor students' learning through their work, providing feedback both written and verbal where appropriate. Make sure your feedback is specific, using the language discussed in the success criteria, and provide strategies that target areas of need.

• Ask students to reflect regularly on their learning both before and after receiving feedback, to describe the strategies they've used to improve based on that feedback, and what they believe their strengths and challenges are. This information can help you determine how to group them for both expert groups and regular grouped activities.

• Hold one-to-one conferences to really understand what students know and can do. Consider distributing a Google Forms survey beforehand that asks students specific questions that not only prepare them for the conferences but also scaffold their reflection process (see Figure 5.1 for an example). Because students will already have had an opportunity to think about what they'll be discussing in the conferences, you should be able to home in on the important details for each student more efficiently. Since Google Forms automatically generates a separate spreadsheet with the answers provided by the survey takers, you can make notes inside this document next to students' responses to keep all the data organized.

• Have students work together in small-group conferences so that you can get a sense of students' collaboration skills as well as specific group dynamics and relationships. Which students hang back? Which ones take the lead? Who works well with whom? You should be able to find answers to all these questions through observations early in the year. It's a good idea to let students pick their first few project groups (depending on the age; younger students may need more guidance to understand the thought process behind choosing effective groups) and then make adjustments as needed as the year goes on.

Develop Rubrics Together

A great way to help students internalize and use success criteria is to allow them to co-create rubrics. The rubrics don't need to be the traditional kind showing how the criteria are fulfilled in several areas at varying degrees of mastery; instead, they can simply show what an assignment that meets the standards should include. I like students to know the specific standards we are trying to cover when we start, so they know what we are working on. Students can analyze the standards, decide what mastering those standards would look like, and then figure out criteria for demonstrating mastery.

Figure 5.1 | Sample Questionnaire to Prepare for One-to-One Conferences

1. What feedback have you received from editors or peers?
Be specific about what you learned.

2. Which standards do you feel the assignment addressed?
Based on the Common Core standards or the ISTE standards

3. Which standards are you meeting or exceeding?
Please cut and paste the standards below.

4. How do you know you are meeting or exceeding these standards?
Please give evidence from your work.

5. Which standards do you still need to work on?
Please cut and paste the standards below. You can also mention specific journalistic skills.

6. How do you know that you still need to work or get help on these standards?
Please give evidence from your work.

Here's how to do it. In small groups or as a whole class, have students brainstorm qualities that an assignment that meets a given standard should possess. Write the final list of qualities on the board and, as a class, decide how each quality aligns to the specific work being done. Make sure to refer to the list continually to help students get used to the language of the list, which will also help them when they receive specific skill-based feedback from you and provide feedback to their peers down the line. Here's an example of a class-generated list of qualities for a 9th grade science lab:

- All elements from the lab are present.
- There is evidence and support from the reading to support the findings.
- The lab is organized appropriately to show the scientific method.
- Steps have been followed so that the experiment is done properly.
- The write-up has all parts appropriately labeled.

Figure 5.2 shows the finished rubric with the success criteria that emerged from the students' discussion.

Once the class has created the rubric, make sure that you provide feedback in the language of the standards and offer strategies to meet the success criteria throughout the process to ensure students are moving closer to mastery with each iteration. Students will eventually do this with one another as well. You may want to provide simple checklists to help students ensure that their work includes all the elements listed. In any content area, students will easily be able to determine whether their work is complete.

Introducing Students to the Feedback Process

Now that students understand and have developed and used criteria for success, it's time to ease them into the process of providing feedback. I like to warm up by inviting students to give *me* feedback: this can be as simple as starting an open-ended dialogue about whether they'd like more autonomy in their learning or asking them to write a creative story that discusses what an ideal classroom would look like. Once students have become accustomed to the process, I move on to introducing and acclimating them to peer feedback.

Figure 5.2 | Student-Generated Rubric for 9th Grade Earth and Environmental Science Lab

Standard	Success Criteria
CCSS.ELA-LITERACY.RST.9-10.1 Cite specific textual evidence to support analysis of science and technical texts, attending to the precise details of explanations or descriptions.	Have at least three quotes from the text that support the ideas about global warming and my argument about it. They will be cited properly.
CCSS.ELA-LITERACY.RST.9-10.3 Follow precisely a complex multistep procedure when carrying out experiments, taking measurements, or performing technical tasks, attending to special cases or exceptions defined in the text.	My lab will show that I've followed the steps in the procedure to support what the text and lab directions suggested. My write-up will follow the specifics outlined in the directions clearly organized and identified.
CCSS.ELA-LITERACY.WHST.9-10.1.A Introduce precise claim(s), distinguish the claim(s) from alternate or opposing claims, and create an organization that establishes clear relationships among the claim(s), counterclaims, reasons, and evidence.	My lab report will include a clear hypothesis that states a claim. After doing the lab, my conclusion will include a claim that relates specifically to the experiment done.

Solicit Student Feedback

Rather than launch students into giving one another feedback, give them a sense of the process by asking them to give *you* feedback. Depending on your class's grade level, consider an activity that solicits students' feedback on the current class and what they would like to see more of. Students often have great, unexpected ideas. Consider informally asking students the following questions when preparing them to co-construct elements of their learning:

- Who is in charge of what you learn? How do you know?
- In what ways would you like to be involved in future learning?
- What activities do you enjoy most, and why?
- How do you learn best? How do you know?

Now shift the focus so that students are thinking about what they want to get out of feedback. Providing feedback is a multitiered experience that starts with listening; when we refuse to answer student questions like "Can you look at this and tell me if it's OK?" and instead ask the learner what it is he or she needs from us—and really listen—we can pinpoint what kind of feedback is needed. Your questions might include

- What exactly do you want from this feedback?
- What do you think are your greatest strengths? How do you know?
- Where do you think you are struggling? How do you know?
- Where do you think you have grown? How do you know?
- Which areas would you like to work on?
- How can I better provide you with the feedback you need? For example, do you need me to write it on the page? Or would it be more helpful to discuss it in a conference?

Try to steer students away from a discussion of grades when justifying how they know they are good at something. Instead, engage them in a conversation that has more to do with applying skills or transferring understanding in different classes and contexts in and out of school.

Much of our work up to this point has aimed to help students become reflective enough to understand their needs, set goals, and assess their current progress against success criteria. Once students can articulate what they need, it's the reviewer's role to listen diligently, asking clarifying questions and offering just the right feedback.

Scaffold Early Peer Feedback

You can now let students dip their toes into peer feedback by offering plenty of low-stakes opportunities for them to provide feedback to one another as well as to you. One way is to participate in a class Twitter chat where students review sample work or articles and work together as a class to tweet different kinds of both positive and critical feedback.

Students in my publications finance class participated in a weekly text-based chat where the assigned articles were directly related to projects the class was working on. They applied what they read to their learning, providing feedback to their own project groups on areas where they could improve. The other two teachers who taught this course and I worked hard to find relevant texts that directly met students where they were struggling. Rather than just be given the answers, the students had to seek them out, first figuring out the questions they needed to ask in order to successfully revise and develop their projects. Because students were developing advertising campaigns over the course of the year, they had to conduct research and apply their learning to various aspects of their projects. Small benchmark projects helped them build their portfolios to prepare for their final presentations as an advertising agency.

Another good way to scaffold the peer feedback process is to have students complete a survey evaluating the work instead of coming up with feedback from scratch (see Figure 5.3 on pages 66–67 for a sample survey administered via Google Forms). The questions would vary depending on where students are in the learning, feedback, and revision processes.

Ensure High-Quality Peer Feedback

Feedback is a term that we all use when we're trying to get kids more involved in the learning process. Unfortunately, feedback is meaningless unless we teach students to be specific. The quality of feedback, logically enough, is the top factor in determining how well students can grow from it. When we take a structured approach to modeling and teaching feedback, students' learning will increase in ways that even they will be able to recognize without help. The following are some tips for ensuring high-quality peer feedback.

Figure 5.3 | Sample Survey to Scaffold Peer Feedback: Satire Movie Peer Review

1. Names of the group members:

2. Title of the movie:

3. Run time of the movie:
   - ◯ Less than 4 minutes
   - ◯ 4–5 minutes
   - ◯ 6–7 minutes
   - ◯ 8–9 minutes
   - ◯ 10+ minutes

4. Do you believe the movie was an appropriate length to tell a complete story with no gaps?

5. Why do you believe the movie was or wasn't an appropriate length?

6. Summarize the premise of the satire.
What was it about?

7. Do you believe the group understands the concepts of satire? Be specific.
Based on what you know about satire, what elements of the movie employ those techniques?

8. Do you believe the group effectively understood and used *Great Expectations* to create something creative? Explain why or why not.
Were elements of the actual text accurate and appropriate?

9. Which of the following standards do you believe the group is meeting?
Check all that apply:
- ☐ R.1.2. Students comprehend elements of literary texts.
- ☐ R.2.2. Students use context to comprehend and elaborate on the meaning of texts.
- ☐ R.3.2. Students interpret, analyze, and critique author's use of literary and rhetorical devices, language, and style.
- ☐ W.1.1. Students analyze components of purpose, goals, audience, and genre.
- ☐ W.2.2. Students generate, select, connect, and organize information and ideas.
- ☐ W.3.1. Students generate text to develop points within the preliminary organizational structure.

Figure 5.3 | Sample Survey to Scaffold Peer Feedback: Satire Movie Peer Review—(continued)

☐ Students make stylistic choices with language to achieve intended effect.

☐ W.5.4. Students prepare text for presentation/publication.

☐ S.3.1. Students analyze purpose, audience, and context when planning a presentation or performance.

☐ S.3.4. Students present, monitor audience engagement, and adapt delivery.

☐ M.1.1. Students understand the nature of media communication.

☐ M.2.2. Students develop and produce a creative media communication.

☐ Students understand the technology and editing process.

10. The students were able to film and edit the movie effectively, showing a knowledge of the technology.

     ○ Yes   ○ No

11. Explain your response to #10, discussing the technical effort of the group.
What, specifically, made it a job well done? Alternatively, what needed improvement?

12. What did you like best about the group's movie?
Please be specific.

13. What do you think could have been better?
Please be constructive and specific.

14. What grade, out of a high score of 9, do you believe this group deserves?

     ○ 0   ○ 5
     ○ 1   ○ 6
     ○ 2   ○ 7
     ○ 3   ○ 8
     ○ 4   ○ 9

15. Why do you believe the group deserves this grade?
Please be specific and base your assessment on the standards (see above) where possible.

16. What feedback would you like to provide to the group?
This will be provided anonymously from the class.

• Make certain that students understand the standards and success criteria before they start the assignment and can articulate expectations of quality work. You can provide or create rubrics, as discussed on pages 60–63, as well as exemplar assignments.

• Give students opportunities in class to practice providing peer feedback so that you can answer their questions the first few times. Make sure that the feedback is high-quality, not just "This is good" or "This needs work." We can do better than that. Students need to understand that feedback should also offer a plan of action that helps them move forward.

• Use a teacher-generated Google Form that provides specific scaffolded questions to help students channel their feedback into areas that relate directly to the task, and then share the feedback from the form with the whole class. In this way, you can review students' feedback and add anything important that they omitted. With practice, students will get better at providing high-quality feedback, and you'll save time by setting up the groups and allowing them to work together while you work with small groups or individual students who need additional help that their peers can't provide. Figure 5.4 shows part of a Google Form with a student's answers collected in response to questions asked about a specific project.

Here are some guidelines for creating the form:
- Make sure to design the form to be specific to what is being asked on the assignment.
- Keep the form short and manageable.
- Make sure that the feedback is anonymous to students, but not to you.
- Give students time to fill in the form in class, and allow the form to be editable so that they can revise their answers later at will.

• Encourage students to confer with one another on assignments, not just you. Using Google Docs is a great way to collaborate with and get feedback from one another in real time because comments on the document are archived even after they are resolved. Be involved while students are working, encouraging them to use the language of the standards to focus their feedback as they review those areas in the text and to provide both positive and critical feedback that helps their classmates to move forward.

Figure 5.4 | Excerpt of Student Responses to Survey: Satire Movie Peer Review

Why do you believe the movie was or wasn't an appropriate length?	Summarize the premise of the satire.	Do you believe the group understands the concepts of satire? Be specific.
The movie addressed all elements that were necessary to the plot. It included character's point of view and all scenes led to another. There were no gaps, everything fell right into place. Adding more wouldn't be necessary and having less wouldn't address everything.	The purpose of the satire was to see Molly and Magwich's back story and how life was like before and after Estella was born. The movie also included the story of Molly and Jaggers and gave the plot a twist by telling Magwich that Molly lost the child, so that Molly could give the baby to Miss Havisham for better care. After Magwich's funeral, Pip and Estella reunite, pouring out all their feelings. Estella then dreams of Magwich, not even knowing that he was her father.	The group understands the concepts of satire because the movie mocked many characters. The movie exaggerated Jaggers's role by making him out to be a complete a**hole, however he remained powerful, just like in the novel. The movie also exaggerated Magwich's role by making him out to be a drug addict and a counterfeiter of money, which explains why he went to jail.
I feel that they fit in everything that was supposed to be fit in and couldn't really be shortened.	It was about Pip, Oliver Twist, and Herbert on a game show *Who Wants to Be a Gentleman?*, which is basically doing certain tasks like picking out the right clothes, dancing, and answering certain questions.	They made Pip very sassy, and they added Oliver Twist into the video, which was funny because he was only in the game show for the money.

• Limit anonymous feedback. You don't offer anonymous feedback, so why should students? The goal is to teach students to stand by what they say and to say what they mean without *being* mean. No one should provide feedback that he or she wouldn't want to write his or her name next to.

• Teach students to ask clarifying questions. Clarifying questions are a great way to shine a spotlight on unclear areas, and they are invaluable to the peer feedback process. They can also be used in any subject area—for example, students can use them as they check whether their peers followed the correct steps in solving algebraic equations or fully analyzed a primary source in preparation for a document-based questioning essay in social studies. Show students what clarifying questions look like, and practice asking them in class so that students know how to be specific about any confusion that arises. For example, let's say you've asked students to assess the clarity of a thesis statement, and one peer reviewer doesn't understand what he sees on the page. He could say, "I'm not sure what you mean by 'The author seems to have a rant against the political system'; can you explain it to me?" This simple clarifying question provides an opportunity for the two students to talk through the ideas and work together to fill in the blanks. You can also teach how to ask clarifying questions by doing a fishbowl activity (a role-play performed in front of the class) where you interview a student and model asking questions, writing down answers, and asking follow-up questions that get the subject to go deeper. You can freeze the scene at any point during the fishbowl to ask audience members to share what they notice.

• Use the data collected from student feedback on a Google Form to create mini-lessons to help students improve their feedback in the future.

• Form expert groups of students who are well versed in particular skills or content, and have them focus on those areas when they review peers' work. Expert groups can change regularly or remain the same all year, and you can work with each group to increase its skill set. Chapter 6 discusses expert groups in further depth.

One simple but powerful tool that can help students in any class ensure they're providing thoughtful, accurate feedback is the "yes-rubric," which includes four gradations: "yes, and"; "yes"; "yes, but"; and "no." When students are evaluating how well a piece of work met the success criteria, they don't need to get bogged down in rubric jargon, they just need to pick one of the four gradations: "yes, and" means the work exceeded expectations; "yes" means the work fully met expectations; "yes, but" means the work partially met expectations; and "no" means the work did not meet expectations.

The great thing about the yes-rubric is its simple, accessible language and format. Seventh grade English language arts teacher Shelly Stephens, who learned about this rubric in a course video published by Laureate Education called *Designing Curriculum, Instruction, and Assessment: Designing Rubrics*, explains:

The "yes-rubric" is really a useful tool for feedback for students to use with one another and for the teacher to use with students. I have used myriad rubrics with language of all sorts, but this one seems to be crystal-clear for students. It would be simple to create a graphic organizer for this. It would look something like this:

Yes, and	Yes	Yes, but	No

I haven't used a graphic organizer because it's so simple to write the headings on a sheet of paper and jot notes beneath. Also, I provide much of my feedback as comments on Google Docs or in face-to-face writing conferences, and that is also how my students provide feedback to one another. It takes a little training to start with what's right (the "yes") instead of what's wrong, but students soon see the value of first looking for the attributes that are expected in proficient writing.

Because feedback isn't associated with grading, the process doesn't quantify students' work but, rather, helps improve it. Givers and receivers of feedback alike benefit. Try placing students in expert groups where their own challenges lie, so they can become more adept at identifying the trouble area in others' work and apply their insights and learning to their own work.

Set Up Classroom Structures Conducive to Peer Feedback

Every classroom environment is different depending on students' age and level of mastery, the content being taught, and the size of the class, among other variables. Larger classes in particular will require modifications and additional steps to the process of introducing peer feedback to ensure that no one falls through the cracks. Smaller classes are ideal for feedback because the teacher has more time to get to every expert pair or group in each class sitting.

This is not to say that a strong focus on peer feedback is impossible in larger classes; the AP Literature class I currently teach is at the maximum size of 34 students. They are all the same age but at varying levels of mastery. Knowing what I know about my learners, I am able to scaffold class activities, group students in meaningful ways, and use technology to check in with them both inside and outside class.

Here are some modifications to consider depending on your class's specific needs:

• Break up larger classes into smaller, more manageable groups. Depending on students' age and level, consider letting them form their own groups initially, and adjust as needed. Because larger groups tend to be less productive when providing feedback, make sure groups have no more than five members. It's OK to have multiple groups working on the same skill if there are more than five students who have the same challenge.

• Change the way the room looks when students are engaging in peer feedback activities. Groups should not be sitting in rows but in circles or around a table to ensure that they can readily talk to and collaborate with one another.

• Allow students to move around the room as needed; at times they may need to confer with another group working on something similar. Give students the freedom they need to get what they need.

• If you have the luxury of a second teacher in the room, consider splitting a large classroom into different spaces so the noise level doesn't get out of control (on workshop days, perhaps; read more on the workshop model in Chapter 6). For some students, too much noise is overwhelming and distracting. If you can't allow these students to move to a different location, think about letting them use a noise-canceling device like headphones that will help them focus during independent work time. Sometimes I let students sit on the floor or in the hallway to help spread out the work.

In addition to taking into account your space and your students' needs, you'll need an easy way to gather data and keep abreast of student progress so that you can adjust classroom instruction accordingly. Google Forms and similar tools allow you to enlist students to help gather the data while making their voices heard. Implementing reflection processes as well as goal setting is another way to make sure all learners know where they are and where they want to be and gather the strategies needed to get there. The better learners know where they are, the better they will be able to communicate that to us, which will enable us to adjust accordingly.

The fact that students are taking charge of their learning doesn't mean that teachers are off the hook for tracking progress and adjusting instruction and project time as needed based on observations and student feedback. As students become more adept at tracking their own progress in ways that work for them and you, you can begin to use less burdensome methods for maintaining data. In Chapter 6, we'll explore how expert groups put still more control into the hands of students.

Reflection Questions

1. In your classroom, who currently determines the success criteria, and how are the criteria shared with students?

2. In what ways do you align feedback with the success criteria? When do you give feedback? If you give most feedback at the end of learning, what kinds of changes might you make to ensure that all students receive feedback throughout the learning process?

3. Given the way your class currently runs, how can you best begin to train students in providing peer feedback?

4. What potential stumbling blocks can you foresee and prepare for to ensure smooth integration of peer feedback in your space?

PART 3

THE NUTS AND BOLTS OF PEER FEEDBACK

6

DEVELOPING AND MAINTAINING EXPERT GROUPS

Mastering a large swath of content or skills all at once is a daunting challenge for students. Much more manageable—especially when done collaboratively—is mastering a specific skill or set of content. This is the foundation of "expert groups," or groups of students who have an excellent grasp of a specific set of transferrable skills that they can then teach to others.

This idea isn't a new one; the jigsaw strategy, which has students split up and become experts on different aspects of the content before regrouping and pooling their learning, uses the same concept. The difference is that expert groups are larger in scope and become a permanent part of the class.

Expert groups are structured around the workshop model, an instructional framework that can be used in any content area. The workshop begins with a 10- to 15-minute whole-class mini-lesson in which the teacher provides instruction and outlines expectations. Then students work for about half an hour independently, in pairs, or in small groups while the teacher circulates, conferring with students as needed. Finally, the class reconvenes for a short share session that looks at what students accomplished, recaps learning, and checks for understanding. The workshop usually lasts a couple of days, but the duration can vary depending on the project and the scope of the learning.

To ensure maximum student growth and engagement and to make expert groups an indelible feature of your classroom, you will need to be deliberate in how you develop, organize, and maintain them over the course of a school year. This chapter explains the process of setting up expert groups, how to prepare students to become experts, how to set up the classroom and determine your role, how to deal with challenges, and how to sustain effective peer feedback throughout the year.

Setting Up the Groups

About two months into the year, once you have a handle on students' areas of strength and challenge, it's time to create expert groups. The first task is to take an inventory of the assignment, project, or workshop and identify the specific skills or content knowledge needed for success. Look at the assessment driving the workshop and plan backward as needed. Then break the skills or content up into chunks that would be appropriate for small groups of students. For example, expert groups in a science class may tackle the different steps of the scientific method, and expert groups in a social studies class may examine different primary documents to be analyzed for a document-based questioning essay.

Make group sizes manageable, with no more than five students in a group. Three or four may be preferable depending on the skills you want to focus on or if you have a smaller class. When determining each group's members, consider group dynamics and select students according to both strengths and deficits. Because student experts will be working together, make a conscious effort to get a mix of students in the group. For example, select one student who already exhibits a high level of competency around the skill, one who is willing to take on the hard work and ask questions, one who is organized, and one who plays nicely with others and is willing to defer to the leader of the group. It may also make sense to include a student who is weaker in the particular skill so that he or she can learn from the group members who have a stronger grasp.

The following is a sample e-mail I sent to prepare expert groups for a writing workshop in my 12th grade English class. The students were about to embark on a literary analysis paper requiring them to select their own text and demonstrate an understanding of the author's craft.

Here are the different feedback groups:

1. Introduction: This group focuses on the title (does it match what the paper is about?) and on the introductory paragraph, looking for context-building ideas that engage the reader. Context is something general that readers can connect with. The thesis section should come out of the context and give the reader a more specific roadmap to the rest of the essay. Also look at the sequence of ideas: whichever order the writer chooses to present ideas in the introductory paragraph is the way the paper should proceed. Finally, the poet and the title of the poem should be addressed somewhere in the introduction.

2. Transitions and cohesion: This group looks at how the author ties ideas together and smoothly transitions from one idea to the next. A sophisticated transition is foreshadowed in the previous paragraph and then led in with the topic sentence for the paragraph.

3. Organization: This group focuses on whether ideas follow the introductory text. Does the paper make sense the way it is organized? Look at sequence, flow, and hierarchy of ideas and discussion. There should be no sudden surprises toward the end of the paper.

4. Analysis: This group addresses how deeply the writer conveys meaning about the text. Each paragraph and piece of analysis should be tied back to the thesis statement. How does each piece of analysis support the overall meaning that the author is trying to convey? How deep is the analysis? The paper shouldn't introduce any point that's discussed only on a surface level; each point should add value.

5. Textual support/evidence: This group examines how well the writer supports his or her analysis with evidence from the text. Did the writer select the best quotation to support what is being analyzed? Does it work, or does it provide only a tenuous connection? Is textual evidence cited appropriately using MLA style?

6. Diction/tone: This group's first task is to review the paper to make sure that it's written in an academic voice—third person objective, absolutely *no* first or second person. Then make sure the tone and word choices are sophisticated. If you notice that the author repeats certain words, please call it to his or her attention.

7. Sentence variety: This group makes sure that the writer switches up sentences and phrasing to ensure good flow and readability. To keep the writing interesting and sophisticated, the writer should use short, medium, and long sentences that begin in a variety of ways.

8. Conclusion: This group focuses on the conclusion. A conclusion should *not* be a summary of what the whole paper was about, begin with a clause like "In conclusion" or "In summation," or simply restate the introductory paragraph. Envision the whole paper as an hourglass: the paper should start wide, narrow in to address the specifics of the text, and then go wide again in the conclusion. The conclusion should leave the reader thinking about the message of the paper.

Make sure to allot enough time in class the first few times that groups meet to observe groups' chemistry and make adjustments if needed. For example, if one group is unproductive because students are too chatty or their personal challenges make it hard for them to work together, a simple one-person swap with another group may solve the problem. Don't tell the students being swapped that they weren't doing a good enough job; instead, tell them that you thought they would be a stronger asset to a different group. That said, try not to micromanage. For example, I don't recommended assigning group members labels or roles; instead, allow students to figure out their responsibilities organically.

Preparing Students to Become Experts

Once you've established the groups and placed students appropriately, it's time to start preparing students to be experts in their areas. First, you'll need to actively demonstrate expectations: for mastery of the skills they're to be expert in, for giving good feedback, and for the aspect of the assignment they'll be reviewing. Depending on learners' age and level, your approach for making sure students are prepared to give feedback in particular areas will vary. One way is to provide direct instruction to the small groups individually. Because expert groups use the workshop model, you can deliver this direct instruction during the mini-lesson segment of the workshop, working with a few groups each day of the workshop at different times. Instruction should be concise and provide real examples to ensure students understand the expectations for how they should use group time.

At first, students will need to consider their own challenges with the skill or content so that they know what they are looking for both in their own work and in others'. Make sure to provide students with reading and research in the specific area they are working on that is appropriate for their level of mastery. Differentiate the materials as needed. For example, consider a couple of resources that say the same thing but in different ways. For my own writing workshops, in addition to sending students a brief explanation of each expert group's role, I taught mini-lessons to the whole class on these specific areas. I also provided resources from the Purdue OWL (Online Writing Lab) and encouraged students to ask specific questions. In addition, while we were setting up the groups, I visited with each small group, gave students time to review their small section of the paper, and answered questions as they arose. Once they're done shoring up their own expertise, students can work together to examine bodies of work found online or in a resource library in the classroom and make a bank of common mistakes or challenges to look for in their expert areas.

An essential factor in the success of expert groups is students' understanding of not only the skills or content they're expert in but also the appropriate way to provide both positive and critical feedback. Students need to make intentional and deliberate choices to ensure that their feedback is worthwhile, and you'll need to model and provide that language first. Students can examine feedback you've provided on similar projects or assignments and make clear connections and assertions about other learners. Because students would already be tracking their feedback from earlier assignments, they can easily refer back to it. They can also make a bank of positive feedback that works better than "Good job" or "This is good," such as "The strong hypothesis fits the formula we've been taught" or "The thesis statement clearly addresses a theme and a particular piece of the author's craft." You can develop and gather similar sentence starters to share with students for future use.

For younger students, consider providing sample feedback for common mistakes, such as frequently spotted grammatical errors.

There is no way to be able to anticipate all of the challenges or situations that can arise around any given topic, so it is essential to follow up with expert groups as well as individual learners to ensure that students are staying focused, truly understand what they are providing feedback on, and continue to provide high-quality feedback. Be visible on workshop days until students know what they are supposed to be doing; you will need to answer a lot of questions in the beginning to help students feel confident in what they are doing. Be patient.

Finally, don't spend *too* long on preparation. Although you may be throwing some kids into the mix before they feel ready, it's better to start sooner rather than later. Learning on the fly is actually more useful than trying to plan for and solve potential issues before they arise. Issues will indeed arise, but that's not necessarily bad. Troubleshooting will be a big part of these groups' success. Allowing students to work out challenges or conflict as a group will help build their problem-solving skills as well as test the group's dynamic.

Setting Up the Classroom and Determining Your Role

Expert groups change the dynamic of learning in the classroom. Once you're ready to start using expert groups, you'll want to set up the classroom to foster student growth and productivity. The way the room is configured, along with the tools and resources you provide, will play a large part in determining students' success. Ask yourself, *What will the room look like? How will students be arranged? What kinds of technology will I need? What will I be doing while students are participating in the workshop?*

Because students are in charge of much of what is happening, you'll be freed up to do a number of tasks that often feel too challenging in a traditional, teacher-led classroom. Your first important function is to observe the class and gather data about what is happening. Notice the conversations groups are having: what are they talking about? Are they working together, or have they assigned different tasks to different people? If a group appears to be struggling, see if there is anything you can do to triage an issue as it arises. Be aware of which students are actively participating and which ones aren't, so you can address them appropriately. You don't need a fancy tool to do this; you can do it with a clipboard and a premade organizer with the students' names on it or in a notebook. Then examine the data and determine any changes that may need to be made. These data will also help you tailor small-group instruction to each expert group's specific needs.

If you have decided that explicit small-group instruction is necessary, you can scaffold or differentiate specific skills for students who aren't getting what they need. The smaller setting allows for more targeted instruction, and you can work with students on problem solving. These small-group instruction moments can be as short or long as you see fit. You can then use the data derived from the small-group instruction to make necessary adjustments to the expert groups or assignments. Make sure to make time to reflect on your observations after leaving a particular group so that you don't forget later.

Some students may require more one-on-one time. Whether conferring about classroom learning on his or her own assignment, group challenges, or specific challenges with the assignment, this short but highly personalized one-on-one time can be invaluable to student growth.

Dealing with Challenges

There's no doubt about it: challenges will arise. As one junior noted, "A downside to peer editing is that sometimes your peers don't really know what they're talking about. I usually ask for help from a teacher when the peer feedback I'm receiving is not helping me at all." According to another 11th grader, "Sometimes students don't really put in the effort and aren't attentive in reading your work. That's when it becomes difficult to rely on a classmate to give you feedback."

Both of these complaints are common and can easily be corrected. Because you'll be monitoring what's going on in the expert groups and meeting with small groups and individual students regularly, you should spot trouble areas quickly and find opportunities to correct common errors or inadequate feedback. If students are really stuck, you'll always be available as backup to the expert students.

Here's a troubleshooting story to illustrate. While working on literature essays this year, we needed to create two expert groups for the same skill—organization—each with five students. The class was quite large, and there was a disparity in skills between the two groups. A few students quickly got the point of what they needed to be doing while the rest floundered, not sure what feedback to offer. Once one of the members of the dysfunctional expert group brought this to my attention, I set up a short lunch meeting with the group members to hash out some of the issues they were having. The main problem turned out to be that they didn't know how to help their peers correct organizational problems. So we looked at one of the student papers together, and I gave students some guiding questions:

- First, look at the introductory paragraph. What does the writer claim he or she is trying to prove, and what is the vehicle for doing it?
- In what order does the writer mention these ideas in the introduction?
- Does this order make sense in terms of proving what the writer is trying to assert?
- If so, go through each paragraph and determine whether the writer followed through on every point stated in the introduction.
- Is there a paragraph for each literary device mentioned? Does discussion of the devices proceed in the order in which they were listed in the introduction? If so, you may want to give positive feedback about how the paragraphs align with expectations. If not, you may want to point out that some of the discussion is out of sequence or that one of the paragraphs seems to belong before or after another.

The papers this group had been reviewing were about four to five pages long, and the students clearly hadn't been reading them closely enough. After we had been working together for a few minutes, I realized that they just needed to slow down and read the papers more carefully. I reminded them that I had made their expert group the largest one by design, so that they wouldn't be overwhelmed and could focus more deeply on fewer papers than students in other groups and provide thoughtful, appropriate feedback. If students didn't have enough material to go on because the paper was unfinished or underdeveloped, I told them they might suggest that the writer create an outline to better organize his or her ideas after brainstorming.

After this initial meeting, we met again midway through the few days of the workshop to make sure that all the members of the group were pulling their weight. I followed up with students in other groups as well and looked at the students' papers on Google Docs to see whom the comments were coming from. Which students were really putting in the time, and which didn't do anything at all? It was at this time I held private meetings with students to discuss any challenges that were holding them back. Because these conversations were private, we were able to be frank and set up actionable plans that I could follow up on to hold them accountable.

Making sure that students understand the true purpose of giving feedback—to help their classmates—is crucial to prevent mean or needlessly negative feedback. Because all students' work is in the pool of work being reviewed, they can usually identify with their peers' sense of vulnerability. However, it's a good idea to put a protocol in place for students to report concerning comments to you immediately so that you can directly address the student who wrote the feedback. I advise reading all student feedback during the first two workshops you run. Being especially attentive during the early stages of using expert groups will help you put out fires before they get out of control, and your proactive approach will help discourage further negative comments. You may also want to tell students to let you know when they receive feedback that isn't particularly helpful; usually, such feedback is characterized not by being offensive but by being superficial, off the mark, or in any other way nonactionable. I have found that most students call ineffective feedback to my attention right away.

A Student's Thoughts on Expert Groups

Now that we've explored setting up and implementing expert groups, let's see what a student has to say about them. This senior in AP Literature and Composition shares her insights on how working in expert groups has transformed her learning experience.

Being involved in groups has helped me learn to adapt to people's different personalities and strengths to elevate the learning environment and produce work that capitalizes on our individual skills. I usually keep my thoughts limited to paper. However, being in a group setting has allowed me to get past my usual habits and grow as a reader, speaker, and writer. Being in groups has acted as a type of "case study" on dynamics between people and has helped to develop my patience and openness to ideas that are not my own.

I have been brought out of my comfort zone multiple times and forced to take on roles unfamiliar to me. Being in groups that have pushed me to take on roles I would otherwise avoid has definitely been a challenge. However, this challenge is what has caused my writing to evolve. I have noticed that I now take on many aspects of a text and qualify my arguments instead of being cemented in one mode of thought. Different personalities bring different perspectives, and I hope to capture this diversity and complexity in my writing.

I have also been able to better understand different approaches people take to completing certain assignments. Understanding people's reasoning and perspectives has allowed me to better understand myself and question my methods. I have become able to adapt to certain groups and grasp a feeling of what work would be possible to produce, what is beyond our limits, what we are willing to commit, and if role changes are needed. Usually I do not like being forceful, and I try to provide feedback in the most benevolent way possible, but there comes a time when I recognize a peer's lack of interest in completing an assignment, and in this instance, I become more assertive. However, in most cases, I am able to provide suggestions that flourish in a collaborative setting where everyone is eager to participate.

—*Barbara Kasomenakis*

Looking Forward: Sustaining Effective Peer Feedback Throughout the Year

Like learning of any kind, expert groups need to evolve to remain relevant and helpful to students over time. For optimal learning, students need plenty of practice coupled with opportunities for growth.

The best way to keep tabs on how things are going and determine what changes you may need to make is to gather data continually. Students should be a part of this process as well, discussing the health of the expert groups through conversation and reflection. You can decide to do the reflection element a number of different ways. Students who like to write can complete thoughtful written reflections, whereas those who prefer other media can consider creating videos, screencasts, audio recordings using a tool like Voxer, or even voice memos on their phones. Some questions for both you and your students to consider include *Are the expert groups functioning as they should?* and *Where are there challenges, and how are those challenges being addressed?*

This section explains how to help students continue to hone their individual expert skills, provides expectations and best practices for ongoing peer feedback, looks at when and how to switch up expert groups, and describes how to incorporate feedback into contexts aside from expert groups.

Further Development of Expert Skills

Although the whole class will learn at least the foundations of important skills and content, students will continue to develop their individual expert skills as they work both in their expert groups and alone. You can help groups home in on specific strategies that will help them go deeper in and out of class. Individual students may also reach out with challenges they're experiencing personally or in their group that they don't believe are being addressed and apply their new learning to their expert roles. Kahyun Kim, an editor-in-chief in training, shares her experiences of growing into a new role:

As editor-in-chief, I read all the stories that the reporters write and make sure that each writing piece follows the newspaper criteria. I also make revisions for grammar and make suggestions to create a better flow of words and content. I try not to change the students' writing too much unless it does not grammatically make sense. For the most part, I am aware of the rules that the newspaper uses. But as I provide feedback, there are some "rules" or "formats" that I am unsure of because (1) I have never written in that particular format, (2) I have never encountered it, or (3) I have never wondered about it. When I come across certain formats that I haven't seen, I ask Ms. Sackstein to see if they are appropriate.

In a way, I feel like a bridge between the students and the teacher. One time, one of my peers asked me if hashtags were allowed to be used in headlines. That was a question I had never wondered about, so I didn't have an immediate answer. I asked Ms. Sackstein if hashtags would be appropriate in a headline, and she said it was fine as long as it was relevant to and talked about in the story. I went back to my peer and explained what Ms. Sackstein had told me.

Through Google Docs and face-to-face conversations with my peers, I help them develop their stories. Sometimes I make comments, proposing different ways to write a sentence or prompting them to attribute a quote in the correct format. When students do not understand one of my comments, they ask me during class, and I gladly help them and explain.

Sometimes I "force" suggestions. For example, because my school consists of both middle school and high school and there are only upperclassman (junior and senior) reporters, student quotes usually come from high school students. If an article is relevant to both middle school and high school—for example, a recent preview of the school's Sports Night, which includes both middle and high school participants—I ask the reporter to get a quote from a middle school student to make sure the article is representative. Also, if I feel that a quote does not have sufficient information to support the piece, I give ideas on some follow-up questions that the reporter can ask the interviewee.

In addition to providing direct instruction and answering student-initiated questions, you can give expert groups exemplars from high-performing expert groups to review. As the groups become more adept throughout the year, the level of the exemplars will improve and your expectations will rise. At first, you will be selecting good work to share with students who are still struggling to provide better feedback. As time goes on, students themselves will share what they now recognize as excellent feedback with struggling members of their expert groups. By allowing students to review new exemplars regularly, whether during workshop time or during directed small-group instruction, you should be able to ensure continual clarity of the process.

Ongoing feedback from students is essential, since the needs of each expert group will be changing as learners grow. Make sure to regularly elicit student thoughts and make adjustments to ensure the expert group process continues to go smoothly, fixing issues before they break down the system completely. Students can submit feedback anonymously to you through Google Forms, so they can feel free to be totally honest about the feedback they are or aren't getting from their peers. Encourage students to be specific about their work in their feedback so that you can target trouble areas and make changes as needed. Here are simple progressive steps to take after identifying a problem with feedback:

1. Observe students regularly during the workshop, answering questions and filling in blanks on the spot and maintaining a log of challenges and areas of confusion that have arisen. Anytime you get a question or notice an area in need of improvement, address it and note it for future reference.

2. If step 1 doesn't resolve the issue, hold small-group interventions where you review the protocol and expectations for expert groups having problems.

3. If step 2 doesn't resolve the issue, hold individual conferences with students to try to triage the challenges, conferring with students in most urgent need of intervention first.

4. Solicit feedback on more specific challenges via an anonymous Google Form that you can use to address issues with the individuals involved or the whole class, as needed.

For example, say your 3rd grade class is working on a math equation, with each expert group focusing on solving the problem a different way, and you notice a student who clearly doesn't understand what's happening in his expert group. The first thing you do is ask another member of the group to explain in her own words how to solve the problem. If the struggling student is still not getting it, then you can work with him one-on-one until he is solid on the learning, move him to another expert group to see if he can find success elsewhere, or invite a classmate to tutor him in the trouble area. After the issue has been resolved, elicit feedback both from the struggling student and from other members of the expert group to see how it's going.

Ongoing Expectations for Groups and Peer Reviewers

Once expert groups become a part of the culture, it's important to provide flexible time throughout the year. Workshop time is purposefully less structured to allow students to ask for what they need when they need it rather than having everyone in the class working on the same thing at the same time. Some students may work on their own, others with a partner, and others in their expert groups. While students are working on projects in class or during any workshop, they gradually develop their particular strengths and gain reputations for being the "go-to" people for certain areas whom classmates can come to for help. To avoid any bottleneck with students who have developed the strongest reputations, gently remind students that others are available to help as well. To prevent students from automatically going to you with questions, implement the "ask three before me" strategy, which I learned about from some elementary school teachers: simply encourage students to ask three different classmates for help on a problem or question before they come to you. This way, students take ownership of their learning and often get their needs met without needing your help after all.

Students can keep logs of which peers they asked which questions and the answers or feedback they received to keep track and know whom to go back to (or not). At no time should a student ask another, "Can you read this and tell me if it's good?" That's a question best reserved for friends at another time. Class questions should be pointed, specific, and easily answered in a short span of time—for example, "I need feedback on my hypothesis as I'm not sure it meets the requirements for the lab project," "Does the evidence for my document-based questioning essay adequately support the thesis I've written?" or "Did I take all of the appropriate steps to solve this math equation?"

Finally, all of this feedback should be reciprocal. Ideally, while one student is providing information, the other is doing the same for a different classmate. If you spot or hear about an imbalance, sit with students one-on-one to find out what the issue is. If certain students continually impede the process or fail to give substantive feedback, you may need to assign them other roles, such as taking the status of the class or monitoring computer usage. Ask students who aren't getting the feedback they need to use the "ask three before me" strategy before conferring with you.

Switching Expert Groups to Enhance Class Dynamics

When is it time to switch groups? your students might ask. Some students may transfer out of groups at your discretion or on their own accord, depending on how you want to establish the protocol. If students ask to switch groups, you may grant the request depending on their reasons and their level of skill. It makes sense to move students who aren't getting what they need in a particular group or who can better serve the class in a different group. Sometimes a student discovers that he or she has a facility in a different area and gains a new sense of enjoyment helping students with that skill. It's also fine for students to stay in the same group all year, developing one skill set very well while improving some of their others.

You may do a wholesale rotation as well. I advise keeping students in the same group for more than one project, but it might make sense to change groups at the beginning of a new marking period or semester, when you're introducing new units. Depending on the data gathered from the groups at the onset of your implementation of expert groups, you can determine whether smaller groups may be more effective given the needs and dynamics of the class.

Again, reflection is essential in this process. Peer experts should consider their level of growth against the standards and, by the end of the school year, be able to demonstrate that growth through their work portfolios and to discuss how they have progressed based on the feedback provided by the teacher and peer experts. Peer experts will continually reflect not only on the work they are doing to serve others but also on how serving others has helped them grow. This articulation will also prove a level of expertise gained from spending so much time on a particular skill area.

Integrating Peer Feedback More Broadly

Peer feedback isn't valuable only in the context of expert groups; it is essential to every aspect of the learning process and can be used in any content area or grade level. Whether the assignment is delivering speeches, demonstrating the scientific method, or presenting the latest math statistics, you can involve students in the peer feedback process and deemphasize your role as the expert in the room. The following are some examples of opportunities for incorporating peer feedback.

• Reviewing content and practicing skills in preparation for a test offers an excellent opportunity for peer leaders to lead lessons and then circulate around the room, helping you provide feedback and answer any questions that arise. This approach can work especially well in math, such as when students are learning how to use different formulas or trying to understand multiple approaches to grasping a concept. Different students may excel at different methods for solving problems; some students may be better at using visual methods, while others prefer to do calculations in their heads or with manipulatives.

• After the test is a great time for reflection and feedback. You can set up peer pairs to go through an exam and figure out where problems arose. Pairing students according to their areas of strength and need will allow for more specific feedback as well as provide an opportunity for students to correct their tests and demonstrate current knowledge in a retest or another kind of assessment.

• During lab time in science class, students can give one another feedback based on the results of their experiments. Lab write-ups, like history papers or English essays, require students to follow a prescribed format and be precise in describing their findings.

• Language labs and classes also require regular feedback. This would be a great opportunity to employ nonnative English speakers as helpers. For example, in a Spanish class, English language learners may be able to help native English speakers improve their accents, their fluency, and even their writing by listening and providing both verbal and written feedback.

Reflection and Development of Skills

However vigilant teachers are, we can't be everywhere at once, so we're often missing a piece of what is going on in our classrooms. This is where student reflection really comes in handy. Give students a role in identifying areas of growth and reflecting on areas of continued need. Consider using reflection in place of traditional exit tickets, giving students time in class to think about what they were able to accomplish today, specific skills they had a chance to work on, and how they can apply those skills moving forward. Making time for reflection in class shows what a priority you place on the process and allows students to really embrace and internalize new learning. By engaging in this practice, students will also keep getting better at pinpointing areas of strength, need, and growth, a skill that will serve them well when they work in expert groups or as peer editors. Identifying others' areas of need also helps them become acutely aware of where they struggle; it is easier to spot inconsistencies or trouble areas in other people's work first and then apply what insights they've gained to their own learning.

Here are some ways to use reflection to help students make the learning connections:

• Scaffold the reflection process by starting with specific prompts (questions) that address the learning in the feedback process and help students know what they should be focusing on. For example,

- What did you notice about the work you were giving feedback on?
- How does this help you see your own work differently?
- When receiving feedback from your peers, when do you know what to use and what not to use based on your knowledge of what actionable feedback looks like, and how does this improve your learning?
- When do you decide to ask the teacher for help?
- Do you tend to always get the same feedback, or is the feedback always changing? What do these two situations indicate?

• Have students reflect on the specific goals they set at the beginning of the project or workshop and how well they are accomplishing them against the standards. As students reach the older goals, have them set new ones.

• Review students' reflections to help you better assess their learning and make adjustments to small-group and whole-class lessons.

• Have students revise their reflections with specific evidence from their work as they continue to learn throughout the process.

For more guidance on teaching students to reflect, check out my book *Teaching Students to Self-Assess: How Do I Help Students Reflect and Grow as Learners?* (2015).

In Chapter 7, we'll look at how technology can support you and your students in the reflection and feedback process.

Reflection Questions

1. As you think about your own curriculum and where expert groups would be appropriate, consider the feedback you currently offer students. Would it be robust enough to provide a model for future expert groups, or would you need to amp it up? How do you know that the feedback you're providing is ample enough? Where would you make adjustments?

2. What is your current role in the classroom? How can you move yourself to the side more? Think about your students. Which ones are strong and have leadership potential, and which require more one-on-one time? How can you meet the needs of both groups of students without losing the kids in the middle?

7

USING TECHNOLOGY TO SUPPORT PEER FEEDBACK

Although technology is not necessary for peer feedback, it can certainly enhance the process. Using technology makes real-time collaboration easier and also allows students to access their learning from anywhere. When students' work is saved on the cloud and accessible via Google Docs, we don't need to worry about them remembering to bring it to school. Technology also streamlines the learning and revision process and provides a safety net: work doesn't get lost, and old feedback or revisions are usually retrievable.

This chapter describes what I believe are the most useful tech tools and applications, explains how to use commenting on Google Docs, discusses how blogging and commenting can strengthen students' feedback and digital citizenship skills, and offers ways to work around technological limitations.

My Top Tech Tools

The following is a list of my go-to feedback apps or programs. This is certainly not meant to be a complete list, but these are the tools I find myself going back to again and again. They're flexible, free or cheap, and easy to use, and—most important—they provide robust support for the feedback process.

• **Voxer.** The Voxer Walkie Talkie app, which can be downloaded for free on students' smartphones, is great for giving voice feedback or communicating when not in the same location. This app also enables you and students to add vocal intonation to feedback, which provides another way to practice communication skills as well as making the feedback more palatable.

• **Screencasts (Screencast-O-Matic, Jing, iMovie).** Screencasts are a great way for students to take ownership of learning and create tutorials for their classmates. A screencast allows the user to capture screens and provide voiceovers that narrate what the viewer is seeing. Expert groups can use this tool when they notice a particular classwide area of challenge. By creating a short informational screencast, a group can provide feedback and helpful strategies to the entire class. Students who receive feedback can refer to the screencast as needed to learn the strategies and apply them during the revision process or even on different assignments moving forward. Over time, a class can assemble a library of these tutorials that students can consult whenever they need to.

• **Google for Education.** Google for Education, which houses student learning on the cloud, is a great platform for student collaboration and feedback. Students with a school Google account have access to a drive where they can compose their work using programs like Docs (a word processor), Sheets (a spreadsheet app), and Slides (a presentation app), along with a host of other applications that allow for real-time collaboration and commenting. I discuss the commenting feature of Google Docs in more depth on pages 103–106.

• **Blogging platforms.** Blogging, a way for students to hone and share their authentic voice, offers an authentic online community-building experience. When students blog in class, they build their digital citizenship skills and practice sharing feedback online. There are many different free platforms available for a range of age levels and with a variety of options like privacy settings. If your school is already using Google for Education, then students have access to Blogger as a free option. I discuss blogging further on pages 107–110.

Some additional apps I like to use include

• **Periscope**, a livestreaming app that allows students who are missing class to see the lesson. It can also be useful for students who need to see the lesson more than once. Expert groups can also use Periscope to share what they are doing with classmates.

• **Skype**, a conferencing app that enables communication among students who can't be in class or in a group at the same time and permits them to participate in the learning virtually. Students can get involved virtually and still participate in the learning.

 • **Twitter**, a social media app for microblogging that is also useful to backchannel learning. Students can use a class hashtag to ask questions and share helpful resources or comment on one another's work. This is also a great way to get more reticent students involved in larger class discussions about the learning.

In addition to getting to know these basic tools, take time to review the newest apps or tap into what students are using on their own and try to bring those into the classroom environment. My students like to use Instagram to virtually share their work and learning and write captions to get other classmates involved in the learning, too. Instagram is also great for drawing in reader engagement in journalism class: for example, students could share a photo and ask followers to write a story caption based on what they see. If you are unfamiliar with the technology, don't see that as a deterrent, but treat it as an opportunity to invite a student to run a Lunch and Learn to go over the new app or tool with the class. You'll learn about a new piece of technology that could support learning in your classroom, and your student will feel an increased sense of agency over his or her learning. Win-win!

How to Comment on Google Docs

By far one of my favorite tools to use in class is Google Docs, which enables participants to review, edit, and comment on documents simultaneously, in real time. Its utility is tremendous: it can be used in any content area that requires word processing. For example, math teachers can use it for logic proofs or algebraic problems, science teachers can use it for lab write-ups or research projects, and English and world language teachers can use it for writing assignments.

One of its most useful functions, especially when feedback is your priority, is the commenting tool. This allows students to highlight specific areas of text and then provide feedback targeted to those areas. The comments, which appear on the side of the document, are linked to the highlighted text. From there, students can carry out a dialogue through the comment box or resolve the comments once the changes have been made. Figure 7.1 shows what the comment box looks like.

Figure 7.1 | Google Docs Comment Box

Using the commenting function encourages an engaged dialogue, replacing the traditional system in which the teacher red-lines or corrects an assignment, essentially doing the learning for students. Students learn by doing, so every opportunity we take away from them to review and revise their work removes them further from authentic ownership.

It's easy to use the commenting function, which users can access three ways: (1) by highlighting the text and then going into the insert menu and clicking on "comment," after which the box will appear on the side; (2) by highlighting text and clicking on a little comment icon that appears on the side of the text (this is a new feature); or (3) by using the shortcut: on a PC, it's Ctrl+Alt+M and on a Mac, it's ⌘+Option+M.

The commenting box appears as a text box that can be typed in directly. All the user needs to do after writing a comment is hit Submit, and the comment affixes itself to the document. The user then has the option to add a reply by typing in the "reply" box and hitting Enter. The dialogue can continue for as long as the participants like. When the owner of the document is finished with the feedback, he or she can decide to "resolve" the comment, which will temporarily delete it from the page. The comment isn't actually gone, however; it can be "re-opened" by going into the Comment menu at the top right of the document (see Figure 7.2). This safety net ensures that the user and the peer reviewer (and you) don't inadvertently lose any of the feedback. Figure 7.2 shows a user resolving a comment and re-opening it.

Figure 7.2 | Resolving and Re-opening a Comment

In addition to the commenting function, there is a "suggesting" function that allows the user to make visible changes, as with Word's Track Changes function. To switch to the suggesting tool, just click on the Comments button on the upper right side of the document and switch from editing to suggesting (see Figure 7.3, p. 106). Once the selection is made, comments will appear as suggestions instead of edits on the page.

When the reviewer makes a suggestion, the owner of the document will be notified and can decide to accept or reject the suggestion. Accepting the suggestion will automatically correct the document, while rejecting it will leave it untouched (see Figure 7.4, p. 106). The reviewer who made the comment or suggestion gets a notification of which choice the document owner made.

Figure 7.3 | Switching from Editing to Suggesting

Figure 7.4 | Accepting or Rejecting Suggestions

Another great Google Docs feature is the ability to "tag" people in comments, which automatically sends an e-mail notifying the tagged people that they have received feedback. All a user has to do to tag someone is hit the "+" and add the person's e-mail address. Once a person has been tagged, the program saves his or her e-mail for future use. Tagging helps students keep track of the work being done and reminds them to check their documents regularly. Students can also tag you in the conversation if they require your intervention for any reason.

Blogging, Feedback, and Digital Citizenship

Blogging and other social media tools like Twitter are excellent ways for students to express and reflect on their learning and transfer it to contexts beyond the classroom. Other like-minded individuals from all over the world will gravitate to share their common or contrasting experiences. As students become more reflective, your classroom's culture of feedback will flourish.

Figure 7.5 shows an example of how I've used Twitter in class to dig deeper into a discussion. I responded to a student tweet with questions that furthered the conversation and promoted deeper thinking. Twitter is a great place to make learning public and provides access to experts in the fields that students are studying.

Figure 7.5 | Using Twitter to Deepen Discussion

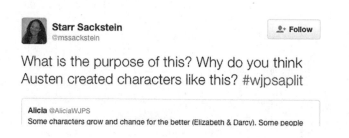

Student blogging is a great way to strengthen digital citizenship while practicing writing skills for a targeted audience. When students publish their writing on a public forum, we want to make sure that they aren't only sharing but are also consuming and providing meaningful feedback to their peers in public, digital spaces. On blogs and social media, most of the feedback and dialogue emerges through comments—a messy arena if not managed carefully. Ross Cooper, the supervisor of instructional practice K–12 in Pennsylvania's Salisbury Township School District, shares some ideas about how teachers can help students engage in quality commenting:

One of the primary benefits of blogging isn't just the authentic audience to which students gain access, but also the built-in structure that allows for said audience to comment on what is read. Therefore, while educators should approach blogging almost as if it is an entirely distinct writing genre, a similar treatment must be given to blog commenting. In other words, teachers should invest the time to explicitly teach students what it takes to leave a quality comment.

The last thing we want to do is simply tell students, "Here's what's included in a quality comment." We must model inquiry by having them "uncover" what is involved. Then, students will (1) have a deeper understanding of why these components are significant and (2) be more likely to apply them.

Here's what this process could look like:

1. In small groups, students explore authentic blog post comments, which should probably be vetted by the teacher ahead of time. During exploration, students separate comments into two piles: (a) good and (b) bad. (You can get more specific by having piles for poor, good, very good, and excellent.)

2. Still in small groups, students dive into the "good" pile. For each one of these comments, students record the features that make it good and attach it to the comment itself through something like a sticky note.

3. Students come together as a class and discuss their group notes along with the comments (evidence) on which they are based. While this conversation is taking place, a definitive class list of quality commenting features is created. After, the teacher ensures that all students understand what has been recorded and distributes and posts the list so that students can access it wherever and whenever.

When a similar process was followed with my 4th grade students, these are the components upon which we decided: proofread before publishing (spelling and grammar), take your time, ensure proper length, be supportive, be honest, be creative, sandwich, begin with prewriting (outline or rough draft), be specific (let the writer know that you carefully read and considered his or her blog post), use constructive criticism, and try to start a conversation with either the blogger or other commenters (asking a question can help).

In reality, quality commenting falls under the same category as teachers and students providing feedback on student work, which, according to John Hattie (2012a), is one of the top 10 instructional strategies for influencing student achievement. So, one option is to explore what effective feedback looks like, and then guide the student conversation to ensure some of this information makes its way into the definitive class list of quality commenting features. Another option could be to administer more direct instruction that hammers home how feedback should be given.

In his *Educational Leadership* article "Seven Keys to Effective Feedback," Grant Wiggins (2012) describes these seven features as goal-referenced, tangible and transparent, actionable, user-friendly, timely, ongoing, and consistent. For a more simplified approach, Hattie's glossary of influences on student achievement states that feedback must answer three questions: "Where am I going? How am I going? Where to next?"

As students learn about feedback, they will be better equipped to apply these practices across all assignments, not just blogging. My students worked in groups for about half of our project-based learning units, and during countless other assignments and activities. As a result of our commenting/feedback-related lessons, they were able to continuously learn from each other, not just from the teacher. In other words, I didn't actually have to be with my students for them to advance their knowledge and move their work forward. Through gradual release and a shift to student-centered learning, they gained the confidence to monitor their own work and one another's.

Consider the example shown in Figure 7.6 (see p. 110), which comes from an AP Literature and Composition student's blog. Students are sharing ideas about what the post connects to in their own experiences, and the dialogue that ensues is respectful and thoughtful. Using commenting protocols like those suggested by Cooper can help students develop their digital feedback skills.

A common misconception is that blogging is just for ELA classes. On the contrary, because it's just a tool to share ideas in a public forum, it can be used to foster discussion of all kinds of issues and topics in any content area, starting as early as elementary school. For example, environmental science classes could blog and comment about local water quality or air pollution, and world language students could blog and comment about events in parts of the world where their language of study is spoken. The possibilities are endless.

Figure 7.6 | Example of Quality Blog Commenting

---

7 Comments

Alyssa Kangx3 September 14, 2015 at 1:25pm

Hey! I can honestly say that how you describe Viola in the play sounds like she's liv-ing the life of Hannah Montana. They both lived a double life and also they tried hard to impress someone. You don't need to fake yourself to impress someone and I feel like a lot of people our age are doing that. They feel they are not much of worth and I can really relate to it. I like how you used a humorous tone while keeping it serious at the same time. It helped a lot to find relations and to get a slight viewpoint of my own on this play. From what you have said, I think I need to double-check on reading this one! Great job explaining a bit about the characters and a few of the major parts of the play!

Reply

Replies

Alyssa Striano September 15, 2015 at 1:36pm

Thank you so much!!!

Once students understand the basic strategies for providing excellent feedback, they should be well prepared to write high-quality comments on social media. As Cooper suggests, commenting on blogs is essentially the same as providing peer feedback on other kinds of learning—with the crucial distinction that it's done publicly. Having an audience can make a writer feel more vulnerable about receiving feed-back. It is important, therefore, to teach students how to be specific and encouraging while not shying away from disagreement—to voice differ-ences in opinion with the goal of establishing a dialogue about ideas, not criticizing for its own sake.

As students learn to represent and conduct themselves online as they would in person, they will naturally develop excellent digital cit-izenship skills. Digital citizenship, which has been a rising priority in recent years, directly relates to what students are doing outside the classroom, even if they don't necessarily connect it with academics. If you model excellent use of feedback via blogging or tweeting questions or conversation starters on Twitter, then students will begin to see the broader applications and begin to communicate with their peers in the same way.

Dealing with Tech Limitations

There are boundless technological tools and programs out there, but not necessarily in your school. Depending on your school's resources, you'll likely need to work within some limitations. If your school permits it, one way to overcome hardware challenges is to implement a Bring Your Own Device (BYOD) policy for workshop days and allow students to use their own devices as learning supports. If any of your students don't have a smartphone, you should be able to obtain a school-owned device for BYOD days, or they can buddy up with a classmate. Otherwise, consider the actual tasks you're having students complete and determine the best non-tech tools to accomplish those tasks.

Fortunately, although technological tools can be fantastic, they're not the only way you can achieve the outcomes you're looking for. You can effectively use expert groups and incorporate peer feedback into your class without the use of devices.

For example, you can set up stations around the room where students can leave printouts of their work that peer reviewers then leave feedback on in different colors to indicate who's providing which feedback. Students can also move around the room during workshop time to confer with one another as needed, privately or in a small-group setting. This setup makes particular sense with a subject like science, where the stations can be used as labs and other learning outlets. For example, if students are learning about the three different classes of rocks and there are student experts for each category, then students can move through the room developing lab work or projects and meet at different stations to gather information. Because students would be experts in only one area, they'd need to network with the other experts to gain information on the other categories.

Regardless of what is being taught, a workshop classroom needs to be flexible. You'll want to set up the room in a way that encourages students to move around. Using tables rather than desks can facilitate a more collaborative environment. You could also create an area where kids can sit on the floor or in a circle area so that they're talking to one another on the same level. If one-armed bandits are the only available furniture, then consider configuring them so that they are in pods rather than in rows.

Another factor to consider in a non-tech workshop is time management. When students and teachers are completely engaged in the work, time gets away quickly. Use a timer or choose a student to be time-keeper so that you can offer warnings when time is running out. Build in reflection or summary time at the end of the period so that students can synthesize what they've learned. They can maintain these thoughts in a notebook and consult them when they begin the next day so that they don't lose time.

Whether we like it or not, technology has transformed the way we think about learning; if we have access to it, we should make use of it in a way that empowers students. As technology continues to evolve, so too must our practice so that we can meet students where they are and help develop their 21st century skills.

Reflection Questions

1. Consider the way you currently run the time you have with students.

2. What does your space communicate about learning? Is it flexible? What can you do tomorrow to help make the space more of a flexible learning environment?

FINAL
THOUGHTS

In a student-led classroom, students learn to depend on themselves; you won't find many students in such classrooms overusing the crutch of teacher support. Empowering students to be leaders and experts doesn't mean you relinquish your own function as educator, however. Rather, think of your role as *reshaped*. Your job is as important as ever. As students assume more responsibility for and agency over their own learning, you can focus on guiding them and developing their learning more profoundly.

Giving and receiving feedback are important life skills that will undoubtedly serve students well after they're done with school. Whether in a higher education setting or a work environment, the self-awareness and communication skills that emerge from reflection and effective collaboration will continue to enhance their growth. Lifelong learners above all strive to progress and become better people, so they will always be eager to hear both positive feedback and constructive criticism.

As we try to promote buy-in for peer feedback among our learners and our learning communities, we have to advocate for these skills and values. Just being able to notice an issue isn't enough; taking the time to communicate it in a meaningful way that another person can hear is important. Students must practice their delivery of feedback, because as important as the recognition of what needs work is the way a person receives it. We've got to ensure that as students share their thoughts, they don't forget that feedback is meant to be useful, not hurtful.

Teaching a student media class has proved to me how capable students can be when taught and then empowered to be in control of their learning. The routines of the newspaper class are so embedded in the work we do that class can function with or without me physically present, which make learning continuous. In an effort to show other teachers that this is in fact possible, I've Periscoped from my classes to give a glimpse inside student learning. A few years ago, I also had some students produce a video promoting the work we do so that other schools could try it out too.

When peering in through my classroom door, others will see me at the side or walking around while the students are moving freely about the room. Each student is working on something different of his or her choosing. At some tables, we have truly collaborative work happening; for example, the web team often sits together, posting articles, communicating with editors, and going back and forth with the fact checker and the photo editor. The students know what they can expect from one another and have a developed a bond of trust and understanding, growing together as a group.

Midway through the year, when we start working with the apprentices for the following year's leadership, the current editors and I sometimes worry that the junior staff won't be ready, but we have to take a leap of faith. We have to trust ourselves and the routines and then just sink or swim. Providing an adjustment period at the beginning of the year is essential, as every team of students will need to make the work flow, the process, and the newspaper their own. And as teachers, we need to let them.

At some point, educators need to take the risk of moving away from the front of the room, putting down the red pen, and stepping out of the chain of command. What's the worst that can happen? Put some faith in students and your teaching, remind kids that you'll always be there to support them, and let the magic happen.

Reflection Questions

1. Where do you seek feedback in your life, and what approach do you take to get it? Do you wait for it to come to you, or do you actively grab it?

2. Consider your students. How can you help them become more thoughtful, aware learners who apply the feedback they receive to their everyday lives?

BIBLIOGRAPHY

Brookhart, S. M. (2008). *How to give effective feedback to your students.* Alexandria, VA: ASCD.

Duckworth, A. (2016). *Grit: The power of passion and perseverance.* New York: Scribner.

Dweck, C. (2007). *Mindset: The new psychology of success.* New York: Ballantine Books.

Hattie, J. (2012a). Feedback in schools. In R. M. Sutton, M. J. Hornsey, & K. M. Douglas (Eds.), *Feedback: The communication of praise, criticism, and advice* (pp. 265–278). New York: Peter Lang.

Hattie, J. (2012b). *Visible learning for teachers: Maximizing impact on learning.* New York: Routledge.

National Governors Association Center for Best Practices & Council of Chief State School Officers. (2010). *Common Core State Standards for English language arts and literacy in history/social studies, science, and technical subjects.* Washington, DC: Authors.

Sackstein, S. (2015). *Hacking assessment: 10 ways to go gradeless in a traditional grades school.* Cleveland, OH: Times 10 Publications.

Sackstein, S. (2015). *Teaching students to self-assess: How do I help students reflect and grow as learners?* Alexandria, VA: ASCD.

Wiggins, G. (2012, September). Seven keys to effective feedback. *Educational Leadership, 70*(1), 10–16.

INDEX

Note: Page references followed by an italicized *f* indicate information contained in figures.

ABOUT
THE
AUTHOR

 **Starr Sackstein** started her teaching career at Far Rockaway High School more than 14 years ago, eager to make a difference. Quickly learning to connect with students, she was able to recognize the most important part of teaching: building relationships. Fostering relationships with students and peers to encourage community growth and a deeper understanding of personal contribution through reflection, she has continued to elevate her students by putting them at the center of the learning.

Currently a Teacher Center Teacher and ELA teacher at Long Island City High School in New York, Starr spent nine years as an English and journalism teacher at World Journalism Preparatory School in Flushing, New York, where her students ran the multimedia news outlet WJPSnews.com. In her current position, Sackstein has thrown out grades, teaching students that learning isn't about numbers but the development of skills and the ability to articulate that growth.

In 2012, Sackstein tackled National Board Certification in an effort to reflect on her practice and grow as an educational English facilitator. After a year of close examination of her work with students, she achieved the honor. She is also a certified Master Journalism Educator through the Journalism Education Association (JEA). Sackstein also serves at the New York State Director to JEA to help advisers in New York better grow journalism programs.

She is the author of *Teaching Mythology Exposed: Helping Teachers Create Visionary Classroom Perspective, Blogging for Educators, Teaching Students to Self-Assess: How Do I Help Students Grow as Learners?, The Power of Questioning: Opening Up the World of Student Inquiry, Hacking Assessment: 10 Ways to Go Gradeless in a Traditional Grades*

School, and, with Connie Hamilton, *Hacking Homework: 10 Strategies That Inspire Learning Outside the Classroom.* She blogs on *Education Week Teacher* at "Work in Progress," where she discusses all aspects of being a teacher and education reform. She co-moderates #sunchat as well as contributing to #NYedChat. In speaking engagements, Starr speaks about blogging, journalism education, throwing out grades (as in a recent TedxTalk), and BYOD.

In 2011, the Dow Jones News Fund honored Starr as a Special Recognition Adviser, and in 2012, *Education Update* recognized her as an outstanding educator. She made the Bammy Awards finals for Secondary High School Educator in 2014 and for blogging in 2015. Most recently, she was named one of ASCD's Emerging Leaders, Class of 2016.

Balancing a busy career of writing and teaching with being the mom to 10-year-old Logan is a challenging adventure. Seeing the world through his eyes reminds her why education needs to change for every child. She can be reached at mssackstein@gmail.com or via Twitter as @MsSackstein. Or find her on Facebook at https://www.facebook.com/MsSackstein.

Related ASCD Resources

At the time of publication, the following ASCD resources were available (ASCD stock numbers in parentheses). For up-to-date information about ASCD resources, go to www.ascd.org. This book relates to the **engaged**, **supported**, and **challenged** tenets of ASCD's Whole Child Initiative; to learn more about this initiative, go to www.ascd.org/wholechild. Search the complete archives of *Educational Leadership* at www.ascd.org/el.

ASCD EDge®

Exchange ideas and connect with other educators on the social networking site ASCD EDge at http://ascdedge.ascd.org.

Print Products

Digital Learning Strategies: How do I assign and assess 21st century work? (ASCD Arias) by Michael Fisher (#SF114045)

Grading Smarter, Not Harder: Assessment Strategies That Motivate Kids and Help Them Learn by Myron Dueck (#114003)

How to Give Effective Feedback to Your Students (2nd ed.) by Susan M. Brookhart (#116066)

Rethinking Grading: Meaningful Assessment for Standards-Based Learning by Cathy Vatterott (#115001)

Teaching Students to Self-Assess: How do I help students reflect and grow as learners? (ASCD Arias) by Starr Sackstein (#SF116025)

DVDs

Assessment for 21st Century Learning DVD Set (#610010)

Giving Effective Feedback to Your Students DVD Series (#609035)

ASCD PD Online® Course

Assessment: Getting Started with Student Portfolios, 2nd Edition (#PD11OC107M)

For more information: send e-mail to member@ascd.org; call 1-800-933-2723 or 703-578-9600, press 2; send a fax to 703-575-5400; or write to Information Services, ASCD, 1703 N. Beauregard St., Alexandria, VA 22311-1714 USA.